DANCE, ARCHITECTURE AND ENGINEERING

Interdisciplinary Book Series
Dance in Dialogue
Series Editors: Anita Gonzalez, Katerina Paramana and Victoria Thoms

The Interdisciplinary Book Series *Dance in Dialogue* critically examines the relations between performance and dance with other disciplines. It fosters interdisciplinary approaches, cross-disciplinary exchanges and conversation as a mode of knowledge production. The series aims to offer new ways of interrogating the relationship of performance and dance – in its broadest conception to include the body, the embodiment and the choreographic – with other disciplines as well as with political, cultural, social and economic issues and contexts. Throughout the books, these relationships with performance and dance are created, presented and theorized.

We seek to challenge the ways in which scholarship has traditionally been represented and disseminated, critically explore the dialogical relationship between theory and practice, and foster the ethos of collaboration, dialogue and political engagement that is needed for vibrant knowledge production both within and outside of academia. We encourage experimentation in publication format and research developed through innovative forms of collaborative and collective working across different modes of disciplinary and interdisciplinary inquiry and dissemination.

To realize this vision, the series offers two distinct publication formats via its two strands:

In Conversation

A collection of short books that present radical thinking emerging from curated conversations between the body(ies)/performance/dance/choreography and another discipline, area of research, field of knowledge or practice on topical artistic, cultural and political issues. Written by leading thinkers (artists and scholars) who critically explore the insights different areas of knowledge and practice offer to one another, as well as the affordances, potentials and implications of these insights for the contemporary world, these approximately 40,000-word books typically develop out of international conversation events and are published within approximately a year afterwards.

Moving Forward

A collection of cutting-edge and forward-thinking, full-length monographs and edited collections that challenge understandings of the body(ies)/performance/dance/choreography and its (their) relation to political, cultural and socioeconomic issues and contexts, foster dialogue and interdisciplinarity and critically explore the relationship between theory and practice.

Other titles in the series

In Conversation titles:
Performance, Dance and Political Economy
Edited by Katerina Paramana and Anita Gonzalez

Moving Forward titles:

The Choreopolitics of Alain Platel's les ballets C de la B: Emotions, Gestures, Politics
Edited by Christel Stalpaert, Guy Cools and Hildegard De Vuyst

FALLING through dance and life
Emilyn Claid

DANCE, ARCHITECTURE AND ENGINEERING

Adesola Akinleye

BLOOMSBURY ACADEMIC
LONDON • NEW YORK • OXFORD • NEW DELHI • SYDNEY

BLOOMSBURY ACADEMIC
Bloomsbury Publishing Plc
50 Bedford Square, London, WC1B 3DP, UK
1385 Broadway, New York, NY 10018, USA
29 Earlsfort Terrace, Dublin 2, Ireland

BLOOMSBURY, BLOOMSBURY ACADEMIC and the Diana logo are trademarks
of Bloomsbury Publishing Plc

First published in Great Britain 2021
This paperback edition published 2022

Copyright © Adesola Akinleye, 2021

Adesola Akinleye has asserted her right under the Copyright, Designs and
Patents Act, 1988, to be identified as Author of this work.

Dance in Dialogue is an initiative developed with the support of the Society for Dance Research
(Registered Charity No. 286595).

For legal purposes the Acknowledgements on p. xii constitute an extension of this
copyright page.

Cover image © Cavan Images / Getty Images

All rights reserved. No part of this publication may be reproduced or transmitted in any
form or by any means, electronic or mechanical, including photocopying, recording,
or any information storage or retrieval system, without prior permission in
writing from the publishers.

Bloomsbury Publishing Plc does not have any control over, or responsibility for,
any third-party websites referred to or in this book. All internet addresses given in this book
were correct at the time of going to press. The author and publisher regret any inconvenience
caused if addresses have changed or sites have ceased to exist, but can accept no
responsibility for any such changes.

A catalogue record for this book is available from the British Library.

A catalog record for this book is available from the Library of Congress.

ISBN: HB: 978-1-3501-8519-7
PB: 978-1-3501-8523-4
ePDF: 978-1-3501-8521-0
eBook: 978-1-3501-8520-3

Series: Dance in Dialogue

Typeset by Deanta Global Publishing Services, Chennai, India

To find out more about our authors and books visit www.bloomsbury.com and
sign up for our newsletters.

CONTENTS

List of figures x
Acknowledgements xii
Glossary xiii

PART ONE 1

1 Landing 3

Togetherness as artistic endeavour 5

2 Dance as conversation with the somatic 9

'Making up dances' and 'choreography' 16
Choreographic dance languages 20

3 Framework: In conversation with 'the literature' 23

Who 'we' are 26
A *Being-in-Place* framework 30
Situation 31
'Mind-ful-body' in transaction 32
Embodiment 36
Identity through the somatic experience of *Being-in-Place* 40

PART TWO 47

4 Chasing stillness 49

Citybody 50
A conversation on waiting 53

People do stop in Waterloo Station: at the top of the escalators! 57
Spatial acts of presence, stillness as presence 65
Weaving ideas – possessing the ground 66
A dance to be made: the poetics of body on *Demonic Grounds* 70
Possessing the street after ballet class 71

5 Lingering in Dwelling, Residing in Wandering 75

A conversation about wandering 76
Permeable, hovering 80
Dwelling and wandering as acts of willing incompleteness 82
Landscapes of opportunity 84
Performance of Self as architecture 88
Hyper-invisibility 94
A dance to be made: *Desire Lines* 97

PART THREE 99

6 *The art of infrastructure*: reflection conversation with John Bingham-Hall 101

The art of infrastructure 102
Ghosts and the unfinished 104
The aesthetic of becoming 106

7 *Choreography as questioning the knowable*: reflection conversation with Liz Lerman 109

Us-ness 110
Sharing 113

8 *Whenness*: reflection conversation with Richard Sennett 117

'Yes-it-is-made' 117
Stillness and silence 122

9 '*I am going to try to be a choreographer in the world*': reflection conversation with Dianne McIntyre 126

I want to try to be in the world 127
'Spontaneous composition' 131

Notes 133
Bibliography 138
About the author 144
Index 145

FIGURES

i   A. Akinleye visual description of relationship between elements of *Being-in Place* and Deweian lexicon, particularly how an *experience* is constituted in *situation*, identity (of a moment, thing, person), and of *transaction* xv
1   Video link for *Choreographing the City* overview film from sharing event at Royal Academy of Arts, London: 28 September 2019. Film: A. Califano. (Hover a phone camera over QR code to be taken to link.) 8
2   H. Kindred and N. Lee, *Choreographing the City: as/at the city limits* sharing workshop (1) at The Place, London, April 2019. Photo: M. Michalowska 10
3   *Choreographing the City: as/at the city limits* sharing workshop (2) at The Place, London, April 2019. Photo: M. Michalowska 16
4   Slide show of images from workshop event at The Place, London, 20 April 2019, along with images from London Bridge, 'hovering' and *Re:generations* performance at The Lowey, Salford, 9 November 2019. (Hover a phone camera over QR code to be taken to link.) 19
5   H. Fulleylove and M Radowska-Judd, DancingStrong Movement Lab.rehearsal July 2019. Photo: A. Akinleye 22
6   A. Akinleye and H. Fulleylove dancing on London Bridge, October 2019. Photo: A. Califano 49
7   A. Akinleye dancing in the street documentation. Photo H. Fulleylove 64
8   H. Fulleylove and M. Radlowska-Judd dancing on the street R&D, July 2019. Photo: A. Akinleye 68
9   H. Fulleylove during stones improvisation and exploration rehearsal, July 2019. Photo A. Akinleye 88
10   A. Akinleye practicing before panel presentation (1), Royal Academy of Arts, 17 May 2019. Photo H. Fulleylove 89
11   A. Akinleye practicing before panel presentation (1), Royal Academy of Arts, 17 May 2019. Photo H. Fulleylove 90

12 Video link to compilation five research and development films, *On Dwelling*, *A Touch*, *Green Version*, *Map Version* and *Whenness*. Films: A. Akinleye. (Hover a phone camera over QR code to be taken to link.) 93

ACKNOWLEDGEMENTS

My thanks and gratitude to all the people who have contributed to this book through sharing conversation, dance and reflections with me over the last two years. I hope I have conveyed the sense of exchange and the shared nature of exploration and creation that framed our conversations, as well as the artistic endeavour that is collaboration. Where given permission I have named you – thank you. I am indebted to Theatrum Mundi for their sustained support of my work. At every turn throughout the process of the book's history there have been acts of kindness, enthusiasm and interest: from strangers joining us in dance on streets, to venues supporting and sharing our work, to friends and family giving feedback on drafts of chapters, to memories of encouragement given to me years before the journey of this particular book began. These moments generosity are such precious gifts and it is the community of these that the book commemorates. Mitakuye Oyasin.

GLOSSARY

Working across disciplines, the written language I choose to use carries with it slight differences of meaning according to the various subject areas. Additionally, it could be language that is not familiar outside the family of texts and artists I draw on! Below I give explanation for choices of language in some of the key words I use throughout the book.

assemblage The elements, that in being together, create something. I could use the words 'grouped together' or 'collection' in place of assemblage but these tend to imply individual things coming together. As I am coming from the notion that we are in *transaction*, creating each other, (all connected, such as in Dewey's 'Hunter and Hunted'), when I use the word 'assemblage' I am indicating that I am talking about the elements of something that connect together through the transactional nature of the lived experience. Thus, they are not separate things – they are the sum of the things.

black, Black, Black-ness The word 'black' indicates a description, while 'Black' indicates a cultural/social identity. I currently cycle around the city. When I am cycling on an empty street I identify as *me*. When I see a woman buying plantain at a local shop, I connect to her through my Anglo-Nigerian upbringing. When I cycle past a man wearing a Jamaican flag T-shirt, I connect to him through us both being considered non-Caucasian. If I cycle past a group of Caucasian men in their late forties talking loudly together, I connect to them through the idea they will see my skin colour as not Caucasian. Throughout my cycle journey my identity shifts, broadens, shrinks as I pass different places and people. 'I' do not change but 'who I am' changes in relation to how I am seen – this affects the speed and direction of my cycling. The colour of my skin and the texture of my hair attracts a position for who I am in other people's responses to me. For the cultural context of how a person is seen or feels in response to event I use Black with a capital 'B'. This is to indicate more than an (inaccurate) description of skin tone. Black becomes a shared set of experiences, histories and responses – a type of cultural identifier that transgresses skin tone. Of course, Black is not a single culture but there is a shared experience of being identified by one's skin that draws on colonization and the history of the transatlantic slave trade. For an interesting discussion see 'The Case for Black With a Capital B' (Tharps, 2014).[1]

When using the word 'Blackness' I am indicating a state of being where I am trying to capture these wider sets of events and histories and social conditions that the identification of 'Black' feeds from, draws on, can be associated with. When I use the word 'black' I am referencing a generalized description of someone's skin colour (that I note here is a generalization for different skin tone ranges).

bodily This is a way to talk about the physical, sense and knowledge that come from sensation. Following John Dewey, I am seeing the world as a matrix of 'mindful body in environment', that we experience as a continuum. The difficulty in explaining that the 'body' is interconnected with the environment and reflective thought is that by writing 'the body is interconnected' I am separating the body in order to describe it as not being separate! Thinking along the continuum of 'mindful-body-in-environment', there are reflections and experiences that are recognized most easily in the muscles and flesh so I acknowledge I sometimes need to write about a sense of 'body' but I do not want to isolate. For this reason, I use the word 'bodily' to indicate the sensation/reflection/understanding that is recognizable in the physical, the flesh, but at the same time by using the word 'bodily' I bear in mind this is not to isolate 'body' as a *thing*. (Also see soma and soma-centred.)

Dewey's language John Dewey's work is best understood as a whole. Where one of his concepts is taken out of context it can be misunderstood. One must remember that he is constructing a *whole* framework. In *Knowing and the Known*, he attempts to explain the lexicon he has used across his work (Dewey et al., 1989). Although he points out that 'in seeking firm names, we do not assume that any name may be wholly right, nor any wholly wrong' (Dewey et al., 1989, p. 7). This anticipates how hard it is to use only verbal language to describe a lived experience which also involves actions and feelings. In this book I use transaction, situation and experience as I understand them within Dewey's work. As with the words so far in this glossary, the language is addressing how seeing the world as all connected often requires a linguistic attempt to use words that indicate we are holding more than one idea at a time. See Figure i for my illustration of Dewey's language along with the notions of *Logic-of-Place* (Pratt, 2002) and Physical Literacy (Whitehead, 2010) which I discuss in the book.

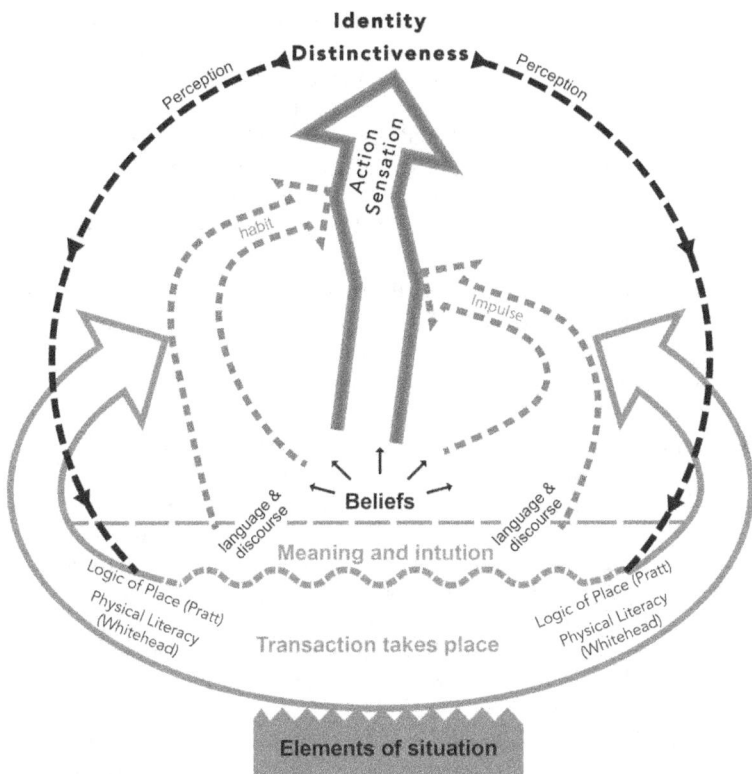

FIGURE i A. Akinleye visual description of relationship between elements of *Being-in Place* and Deweian lexicon, particularly how an *experience* is constituted in *situation*, identity (of a moment, thing, person), and of *transaction*.

experience An 'experience' in the Deweyan lexicon defines an event with specific elements, so not all 'experiences' are Deweyan *experiences*. Dewey gives characteristics that he called 'formal conditions of an aesthetic experience'. These are continuity, cumulation, conservation, tension, anticipation and fulfilment (Dewey, 2005; Jackson, 1998).

> *we have an experience when the material experienced runs its course to fulfilment . . . is so rounded out that its close is a consummation and not a cessation. (Dewey, 2005, pp. 36–7)*

Every 'experience' is unique, the reason for this must be in part because it is informed by past experience and, therefore, one enters the new experience in a different way than one entered a previous experience. Dewey talks about the unity of quality an experience holds. The experience is defined and located retrospectively; experience exists in reflection but it should not be thought of as the property of the reflector, in other words experience should not be internalized as if belonging to only one part of the mindful-body-in-environment. Experience is the uniqueness (assemblage) of the event, the engagement of 'mind' (action), 'body' (sensor) and 'environment' (natural world). It is in the *situation* that experience exists.

situation A *situation* can be seen as the sum of the elements (the assemblage) that engender an experience. The elements come together through transaction. *Situation* can be described as 'container' in which the action (transaction) is happening. Container itself is made up of the elements in transaction.

transaction Transaction has been explained through a number of food analogies. Sullivan uses the analogy of the melting pot, tossed salad and stew. Dewey was not saying that transaction is like a melting pot where all the ingredients constitutionally absorb into each other and disappear, nor is transaction like a tossed salad where the ingredients – although integrated with each other – are essentially just side-by-side (Sullivan, 2001). Transaction is best described as a stew where elements have effectively changed each other but have not disappeared into one conglomerate (Sullivan, 2001). Transaction describes the idea that things constitute each other.

I offer two personal analogies I have developed in order to understand the notion of Dewey's transaction. Firstly, in terms of dance work: light and dancer on stage. The light needs the form of the dancer in order to be recognizable, just as the dancer needs the light in order to be recognizable; there is a transactional relationship because as dancer and light transact their form is created.

My other example follows the use of food referenced above but from the perspective of experience in the mouth (taste, smell and texture), rather than what it looks like. Transaction is not the eggs, flour, salt and sugar in the mixing bowl. It is the taste of the batter pancake they make. I can detect all the parts within the overall taste of the batter but if more of one is added I can taste or feel the addition; if something is taken away, I can taste that also. The parts independently affect the batter, but it is the formula of all the parts that creates the taste itself; salt alone would not make a batter pancake, yet I am fully aware that salt is present. The batter pancake is all the things and all the things have their own taste and affect in the batter.

dif-ability, dif-abled This is a term I am using to indicate the notion of differently-abled bodies rather than disabled bodies (which implies one is defined by a variance from the 'norm'). Acknowledging *dif-abled* is also poignant as many urban environments offer a design that create an inability to move around for some people. However, someone considered to have a mainstream 'normal' body would find it hard to keep up in an environment designed for wheelchair users. It could be seen that designed environments are created without consideration of range of movement needs and then those who the environment ignores are given the identifier of being unable/disabled to engage with them – a self-fulfilling prophecy.

emplacement, embodiment I use the word 'emplacement' to describe 'embodiment' with an emphasis on including the role of environment (or *Place*) in the feeling of 'embodiment'.

In 'From embodiment to emplacement: re-thinking competing bodies, sense and spatialities', Pink (2011) draws on Casey (2009) and Ingold (2000) to suggest a rethinking of what we mean by embodiment to recognize more overtly the integral role the environment plays in the embodied experience. She questions the use of the word 'embodiment' and offers 'emplacement' as a word that better captures the meaning. This raises the question as we orientate understanding and meaning away from dualist notion towards embodiment, do we reappropriate familiar language or associate meaning with new words? This is the dilemma that Dewey faced as he used familiar words such as 'experience', 'situation', 'object' but within the meaning of his lexicon which he has to go to great lengths to explain in *Knowing and the Known* (Dewey et al., 1989).

Howes (2005) calls for a move within the paradigm of the somatic away from the concept of embodiment to emplacement in order to underline the importance of *Place* in the matrix of experiencing Self (Pink, 2011). I am interested in how emplacement underlines the neglect of environment when we discuss experience as embodied. Howes (2005) gives context to embodiment/emplacement when he suggests the opposite to embodiment is disembodiment, the opposite to emplacement is displacement (Akinleye, 2019b, p. 42).

The deeper implication of the use of emplacement suggests that often, when we research or discuss embodiment our focuses imply this is research about expressing or feeling with the *body*, when because of the nature of embodiment, it is research about *Place* of which the body is an integral part but not in some kind of isolation. The challenge is to move beyond a theoretical understanding of the concept of 'embodiment' and find ways to acknowledge the spatiality (the relationships we have between perceived things). There are lessons to be learnt from Native American and other Indigenous cultures that Pratt references as he demonstrates a historical and on-going Western resistance to location of Self spatially, as *in relationship with*.

foregrounded I use this word in place of 'focus on' or 'forefront'. I like to use the word 'foreground' because I am also playing with the idea that grounding something gives it focus. Because of the way the word includes 'ground' I hope it gives a sense of something being empowered through connection (grounding) rather than through being brought to the front (which implies a hierarchy).

historied I use the word historied to acknowledge that the past can shape the identity of a person on a thing experienced in the now. This is to try to collapse the sense that the past is not present in, nor does it shape, the now or the future.

histories I use histories as a plural to acknowledge the multi-layered experience we have of events, therefore, what is remembered and retold is not a single story (a single history), but is the combination of all the perspectives highlighted by different people's experiences of the 'same' event. Using the plural also acknowledges events' meanings and importances differ according to time period, geographic location and cultural background. This challenges a single colonial, Western narrative of history.

incompleteness I am using this word to mean not 'closed off', but still able to be a part of a response. For me this is different from unfinished. The difference between incompleteness and unfinished is a philosophical question I explore in this book. I think the exploration of this difference is interesting and worthwhile (rather than the solving of the difference).

knowledges A combination of knowing different things in different ways. The 's' on knowledges indicates there are multiple ways to come across, engage with and absorb understanding.

moment(s) I am using the word 'moments' because in engineering these are places where weight manifests as a force not having equal or opposite force along its line of action. Thinking temporally (in terms of time/rhythm) a moment is a parcel of time that identifies an experience or action happening. I like to play with this dual meaning: drawing on the engineering use of *moment* when I use the word. I could also be identifying an experience or action as a 'moment' in terms of a particular parcel of weight (spatially/in relationship). My playful use of this word means that the moment I kiss you is as much a point in time as it is a point in the relationship of the weight of my body reaching out to yours in space. I am not aware of this dual use of the word in general.

space, Place I use the word *Place* to indicate the interaction of mindful-body-in-environment. I use *Place* following Dewey's account of *transaction* along with Casey's (2009) use of the word *Place*, and Pratt's *Logic of Place* (2002): *Place* is the specifics of a situation with a spatial perspective. I use *Place* to indicate the transactional nature of a location (which includes the social and cultural element of experience as well as geography and time). I use a capital 'P' to indicate this is a particular use of the word *Place* as the *thing* of all the parts that make the situation.

Dewey's use of *place*, location and situation and Vygostsky's use of *social space* appear to mirror each other and oblige us to think more widely about the role of environment, setting in learning (education). The convergence highlights a theme in work by Dewey and Vygostsky on place/social experience and place/social interactions effect on Self. This returns us to the bodily as the vehicle of knowledge, through which *place, location, situation* and *identity* are engaged with. The word *Place* is used as an above symbiotic linking of 'mindful body in environment' highlighted by Casey (2009), Massey (2005), Pink (2011) and Pratt (2001, 2002) as well as an acknowledgement transaction (Dewey, 1958; Dewey, Boydston and Toulmin, 1984; Dewey, Boydston and Lavine, 1989). Also see *emplacement* above.

I use the word 'space' only when I have to discuss a geographic measure (a theoretical idea of a location). As I discuss, space and time cannot be separated from an embodied perspective to be in space, I need to also be there in a time. To be in time I need to also be somewhere in space. As with body (above) I want to use words that do not isolate any part of the matrix continuum of 'mindful body in environment'. I use 'space' when I have to (theoretically) isolate a part of the matrix.

polyrhythm Making use of more than one idea, rhythm simultaneously. Differing rhythms, ideas, flows can be experienced together as an assemblage.

Self, mySelf I use Self with a capital 'S' when I want to indicate the expansive connected *Being* of a person. The person as part of the constellation of experiences they have that shapes them.

site/sight I use both words simultaneously at points in the text to acknowledge the physical presence of something (sight) and the theoretical presence of something (site) are not separate from each other but different entry points along the continuum of presence. McKittrick also uses site/sight in her work (McKittrick, 2006).

somatic, soma-centred, somatically, somatic-based, corporeal As noted in the discussion of the word 'bodily', I use soma, soma-centreed and somatically all to indicate a sense of the knowledge of something that is recognizable or noticed most easily in the physical sensation of the flesh (bodily). I am attempting to talk about the bodily without separating the 'body' as an isolated thing.

I use the word 'corporeal' only when I mean the tangible touchable flesh part of the Self.

temporality To do with time.

use of hyphens There are places where I string-words-together using a hyphen. I make use of hyphens in order to denote something that is the combination (assemblage) of all the words linked together by the hyphens. I am trying to suggest thinking of the result of all these happening with each other.

I use a '/' such as 'site/sight' when I am offering either or both routes through the sentence.

use of 'ness' (**nowness, whennness**) I use 'ness' in places where I want to also express the ongoing experience. Therefore, I add 'ness' to words to indicate the state or condition of being in that word. 'Now' seems to be a moment that can pass, 'now-ness' is the experience of the state of that a moment.

use of [. . .] I explain this in the main text of the book also. It is the un-verbal element of experiencing as sense of bodily Self.

PART ONE

This book explores *Place*-making from the perspective of my choreographic dance practice in conversation with architectural and engineering practices. The book comprises essays, choreographic images and poems informed by verbal and movement *conversations*, carried out primarily in 2019. This includes activity that took place during the project *Choreographing the City: as/at the city limits*[1] which took its starting point from the paper 'Choreographing the City: Can dance practice inform the engineering of sustainable urban environments?' (Bingham-Hall and Cosgrave, 2019). The activities and events that the book draws on involved site visits to architectural and engineering organizations working with city-scale projects, two week-long residency events where I worked with dancers, musicians, engineers and architects to explore and exchange movement ideas, along with seven public events of performances, sharing workshops and dance/talks.

In Part One, I begin by establishing a framework for the conversations that inform and are featured in this book. These conversations are both movement and verbal interactions. To give these exchanges a context, Part One explores the connections between the materials of *body* and *city* that we (choreographers, dancers, architects and engineers) are working and expressing with. I suggest a common ground of interconnectedness across these practices in the notion of *Being-in-Place*. My hope is in offering a *Being-in-Place* framework, I scaffold the subsequent sections of the book, as well as contextualize the conversations with the literature and artistic creations we have built our respective practices around. Textured by the intraconnected paradigm established in Part One, Part Two is made up of a collection of essays, poems, choreography and dialogue drawn together through the movement and verbal conversations of *Choreographing the*

City: as/at the city limits. These are organized by two themes that emerged across the events: *Chasing Stillness* and *Lingering in Dwelling/Residing in Wandering*. The final section, Part Three, consists of summarizing reflections which were compiled after individual conversations about the manuscript for this book with John Bingham-Hall, Richard Sennett, Liz Lerman and Dianne McIntyre.

1 LANDING

Sitting in dance and reaching beyond the isolating notion of 'subject areas' my choreographic dance work looks at spheres of inquiry into the interconnectedness of *Being-in-Place*. My ongoing interest in this is to explore emerging languages for movement that connect to ideas shared across the collaboration of dance-making (choreography) to building/city-making (community). I believe dance as a field contributes to larger discussions within a range of disciplines that engage with movement and the *Place*-making that dance choreography can also create. Words such as *rhythm, flow, relationship*, are shared vocabulary about structure, self and space, beyond dance. Words whose meanings differ only slightly but whose delicate differences can inform across subject areas and edify the spaces we create together. In conversation across practices, collaboration can offer unexpected perspectives gleaned from the problem-solving approach of another discipline. Fixed positions within the expectations, classicisms and habits of a given practice can become camouflaged and invisible limitations that constrain progress within the familiarity of one's own practice community. However, these positions are discovered by those outside the practice as noticeable phenomena, peeling habit away from practice, so that they can be questioned, deliberated on and reconfigured.

Within dance culture, the sensorial can become a habit, a singular type of body can become the trope of 'dancer', and that body can choreographically explore the same questions again and again (particularly across the culture of mainstream, funded dance projects). Collaborating with other disciplines (such as architecture and engineering) offers new perspectives on the body in space purely by seeing one's own practice through the values of another. Similarly, interdisciplinary inquiry with dance offers urban design alternative evaluations of bodies in space and time. For instance, engineers habitually find themselves in the fixed position of surveyor of the environment they are trying to understand. This leads to evaluating the potential of a location from a single, fixed vantage point physically, but also socio-economically, looking at potential from the single vantage point of being heteronormative – white-male-and-waged (McKittrick, 2015).[1] The collaborations with dance described in this book offer urban fields of architecture and engineering an exploration into sensorial reflexivity to explore the physicality of the position from which they survey – to be somatically and sensorially reflective. It could be that this kind of reflexivity is lacking in practices outside of the culture of dance. These certain kinds of bodily awarenesses within the approach of '*to dance together*' can support the development of bodily/sensorial intelligences in urban design, architecture and engineering.

Dance has only recently come into academic focus as a site for meaning-making with the potential to uniquely understand wider social and philosophical implications (Manning and Massumi, 2014). The moving body as a kind of sociology of embodied experience has '*warranted relatively little attention in academia*' in the past (Thomas, 2003, p. 28). Physical culture and dance philosophy scholars such as Maxine Sheets-Johnson (2009), Brenda Dixon-Gottschild (2003) and Ian Wellard (2015) inform ongoing debates about the role the moving body has in the engagement of Self in world. This articulating and valuing the significance of where Self begins, or ends, or is continuous in environment that dance choreography explores, shares inquiry with colleagues in architecture and engineering (see Pallasmaa, 2005; Rasmussen, 1959), social sciences (see Deleuze and Guattari, 1983, 1987; Sennett, 1994) and geography (see Lefebvre, 2004).

From Foucault (1979) to Bourdieu (1990) it is clear that care for, and regulation of, the moving body are associated with the rights of the individual.[2] Thus, in Western society, the 'body' has come to represent the citizen. Twenty-first-century questions about how we live together after European colonization and in a globalized world are highlighted through how our bodies are free to move – a freedom of movement that extends from the bodily expression of the gesture of a danced step to the ebb and flow of navigating a city, to the borders and boundaries of nationhood and the regulations of movement in light of pandemics. Tracing, designing for, and controlling the moving body mediates how the lived *every day* is experienced. The means by which we notice and language our bodily experience becomes instrumental to the processes we use to understand ourselves, our neighbours and our environment (Lerman, 2011). The cartography of our understanding of the bodily experience directly maps the grace of ourselves in the city. How urban spaces unwrap themselves into the lives of the individuals who reside in them becomes the dance of the city.

Conversations between dance-making and city-making practices involve looking at how accounting for the everyday bodily experience of movement of the city speaks to dance and through dance. Part of my interest in this is to explore the choreography of a *new geography* (McKittrick, 2006) by considering the poetics of female and non-white city bodies. I pay particular attention to how dance-making and city-making cultures engage with the complexities and experiential knowledges drawn from female bodies and non-white bodies in the early twenty-first-century era of #MeToo and Black Lives Matter. By bringing choreographic-thinking approaches to architectural and engineering problems, interest in how a wider and more imaginative range of possibilities of who 'we' can be and what community can become is made available. It seems that through collaboration with choreography, architecture and engineering practices are offered approaches and responses to discussions on aspects of identity, the somatic and movement possibilities for articulating the lived experience of being present in a *Place*. Urban design questions of how the 'ordinary person' is facilitated in experiencing the *dance* of the city are underpinned by choreographic questions of what understandings in and about the body, weight and shape contribute to designing spaces that support the identities of the people who dwell in them.

In Part One of this book, I give a sense of *landing* in dance and the city through discussion of the terms and frameworks that network through the interdisciplinary 'field' of *Place*-making (choreography, architecture and engineering). As such, here in Part One, I engage in conversation with practices and literature to construct a starting framework I call *Being-in-Place*.

Togetherness as artistic endeavour

Dancing

Eyes closed in the semi-dark studio, at the beginning of the dance Charlie and I are each tasked to softly move from one side of the room to the door on the other side. There will be a point when we meet but in this structured improvisation we do not know when that point will happen. As I dance, I move the muscle and bone of mySelf which is defined by the sensorial collision of beyond-me: the texture, force, compliance, breath of the room and Charlie. The walls, floor and Charlie are the expansions of my skin or the moments when my skin is realized –

my limitations and the extensions of me simultaneously. On one leg leaning into the wall on the opposite side of the room from the door, my blood is cooled by the concrete brick as it engages with the palms of my hands to balance my weight. I feel the wall as it reaches in to becoming a shiver in my back. The hairs down my spine extend into the opportunity of movement that is the empty space of the room behind me. A shadowless sensation opens the muscles of my back as the weight in my arms succumb to the walls, sliding me slowly down to where the spongy linoleum of the dance floor welcomes the percussion of my knee, and then thigh and then hip. Legs folded out into the space of the room, ribs opened onto concrete, side of my head caressed against the wall, sitting curve-like into corner of wall-floor, I sigh into the position we – wall, floor, breath and bone – have temporarily made for me. And as I suck air back into my lungs, I swallow the taste-like panoramic faintness of the smell of Charlie, then feel warmth of him gently brush across my extended calf. Eyes still closed, arm outstretched to embrace the floor, I expect to almost hit Charlie, but the indication of his presence is felt only in the sound of his exhalation, and the remembered momentary connection of the brush of my calf. I marvel at how he is everywhere and nowhere around me; I embrace the linoleum for holding me, kiss the wall with my cheek as I begin to move away and encounter mySelf everywhere of this room. Dancing in here, with wall, floor, breath of space, Charlie, the occurrence of 'me' is succeeded by the happening of 'us'. Dancing is the moment of real-izing us: Mitakuye Oyasin.

A. AKINLEYE, *reflection from rehearsal of '. . . Whispers.'*
Choreographer Helen Kindred, November, 2019

From experiences of performing improvisations such as this one, like other dancers, I am practised in the togetherness of space/person/negotiation from the physical perspective of movement with the imagined, concrete, hoped, historied – everything of this moment. Throughout this book I have indicated this *everything* by writing [. . .].[3] The [. . .] 'is the bodily sense that is a person's situation, which is to say, her interaction with the world' (Sullivan, 2001, p. 48).

The embodied moving starting point that dancing can illuminate makes dance, as a field of knowledges, an interesting collaborator across a range of subjects – in the case of this book, city-design practices. As dance taps the [. . .] and reaches out with it in response to interdisciplinary invitations to collaborate, we are mutually offered the opportunity to liberate ingrained principles across practices. This should not be a retrospective rebuking or challenge to ingrained-come-orthodox approaches within a practice.

Rather interdisciplinary work offers collaborating practices the opportunity to be present in and expand into the *now* of the twenty-first century. This book dances into conversation with architects and engineers to better understand if reflective practices within dance and choreography provide alternative forms or underexplored perspectives for engaging design with environment.

For dance, this is also about the reflexivity of noticing the knowledges in the practices of dancing beyond their aesthetics. How we open up our dance practices, ourselves, and what frameworks we need to do this meaningfully gives dance the challenge to 'bring the body to the table' across disciplines in which the body has been marginalized as a shell for the mind. How the perceived mind and body are in togetherness in dance offers larger lessons in collaboration. Thus, dance as part of an interdisciplinary landscape challenges us to question and find methods for how we think-move together in the significance of the twenty-first-century moment.

Almost a quarter of the way into the century, this is a moment charged by a global political climate grappling with how we progress the process of post-colonial healing, in the rush of globalization and environmental devastation. The opportunity to explore, the personal non/pre-verbal of [. . .] and the unfamiliar of difference, through how we pay attention to the *otherness* of another practice offers a mode through which to better understand the context of where we are more generally in the societies we live in. The goal of interdisciplinary work should be to extend context. This work offers reflection and re-imagination of what is creatively possible to manifest, informed by the different perspectives of practices in conversation with one another.

Dancing together engages knowledges that manifest in the ability to *all move around to create something together*. In the togetherness of interdisciplinary work with city-makers, dance offers skills and provides strategies for the physical and metaphorical shaping of space. This book takes an approach to interdisciplinary work that challenges the assumption that it is about looking for sameness as an indication of the possibility of togetherness. A hunt for sameness can become a 'cul-de-sac-ing' activity of logging similarities between dance and city design. Rather, interdisciplinary work is most valuable through its revealing of contingencies of difference. As John Dewey (1958, 2008) reminds us, preoccupation with finding sameness assumes a fundamental and untraversable starting point of difference. Beginning with *Mitakuye Oyasin*,[4] as a principle rooted in embodiment, and following Dewey's Pragmatism, I suggest an assumption of networked connection (sameness). Perceived difference is then a highlighting of the wonder of variety within that connection. An ontology of life as an immeasurable assemblage that is so vastly interlinked encountering it from different perspectives and practices illuminates it further. Then, inspiration is derived from the stimulus of noticing the connections made, and the gaps of difference they appear to bridge when a practice in dance and choreography is in conversation[5] with practising architects and engineers.

FIGURE 1 Video link for *Choreographing the City* overview film from sharing event at Royal Academy of Arts, London: 28 September 2019. Film: Anton Califano. (Hover a phone camera over QR code to be taken to link.)

2 DANCE AS CONVERSATION WITH THE SOMATIC

> A word . . . The meaning of the thing is made up of experiences of its active uses . . . utterance and situation are bound up inextricably with each other and the context of situation is indispensable for the understanding of the words.
>
> **(OGDEN AND RICHARDS,** *1989, pp. 307 and 321)*

> What do I mean in the word 'dance', when I reach-up and pluck the air into a spin or balance on my left leg until gravity peels my foot from the ground in a tide of craving weightlessness – caught by the infinite breath coiled in the spring of my right knee as I step into the sound of a note of music. What is leftover or left out by weaving the momentary-everything of moving in nowness into a word – 'dance'?
>
> **(A. AKINLEYE,** *reflection March 2019)*

The phenomena of dance differs across cultures, generations and social structures (Jonas, 1992; McFee, 1992). An embodied experience, the notion of dance relies on geographic location, historical period and aesthetic preference. Because of this, the meaning of 'dance' is quite individually interpreted, particularly by those coming from disciplines outside of the field. What dance means to a collaborator is often dependent on their personal (non-professional) experiences. Within the dance field, McFee (1992, p. 15) argues that any definition of dance would be so subjective as to be of little use in terms of understanding its meaning. Therefore, rather than attempt to define dance, 'dance' is used here as a term that describes a field of endeavour whose boundaries fluidly respond to cultural, generational and social structures. It is at these fluid boundaries that interdisciplinary work thrives because at these edges, dance can be about somatic response rather than rhetoric of tradition.[1]

Within this fluidity of dance, the dancer's *felt* experience is central. Dance appears to demonstrate the embodied, the [. . .], emplaced experience of simultaneous physical, uniquely and reflectively in transaction with environment. The bodily nature of dance means dance is neither subject nor object (I-am-dance-and-I-am-dancing-and-I-am-a-dancer).

FIGURE 2 H. Kindred and N. Lee, *Choreographing the City: as/at the city limits* sharing workshop (1) at The Place, London, April 2019. Photo: M. Michalowska.

Any construction of dance is temporary and contingent. By the nature of the creative process a re-evaluation of the understanding and knowledges of dance should take place every time it is engaged with (in every technique class and every rehearsal at best, at the end of every project at least). However, it is important to offer the locator of dance I have been using when in movement and verbal conversations with architects and engineers. Therefore, this following construction of dance is offered in terms of being for this project only, these conversations, this exploration.

I have hypothesized dance as falling into two temporally/historically based types: classical/traditional dance, and contemporized dance. The first temporal condition of classical/traditional dance is typified by having been done for a hundred years or more. Although nuances such as the stylized steps, the addition of movements and current commentary might have altered its execution slightly, nonetheless this type of dance stems from locations in time/space that are considered heritage or historical, no longer experienced. As such, this kind of dance carries within it a reference to discourses and social expectations that are situated in the past or in our imagination of what the past was. The classical/traditional type[2] has also been informed by a number of individuals who have passed the dance down. Because of this, this kind of movement becomes 'dance' contingent on cultural or historical context.[3]

The second temporal condition, *contemporized dance*, usually stems from a specific individual's exploration of movement. This area of dance is culturally and aesthetically specific to the individual who initiated it.[4] *Contemporized dance* has the flexibility to respond more readily to discourses outside of its field. It is dance because it is an informed physical expression created by an individual moving with aesthetic, physical intent. It is in this type of contemporized dance that the dancing carried out during *Choreographing the City* conversations resides.

However, the warning associated with *contemporized dance* is that although it is responding to and being created by a sense of current time, it is easy to forget that it is still a retort to the particular places in which it is being carried out. It is not cultureless or socially neutral – it reflects the bodies and contexts of the identities of the people doing it.

My typology of *contemporized dance* should not be homogenized into a general post-modern Western identity. Given this, I look for ways to be attentive to my own body when dancing and encourage others to consider this attention to 'Self-in-body' as an integral part of finding their unique relationship with dance. Part of 'me-dancing' involves an awareness and sensitivity to how *I am* in a considered, somatic feedback loop of being present. Identifying as Black and female, for me, part of the feedback loop is often characterized by a resistance to be marginalized within Western modernity constructs for how I can move and what I should look like. The typology of *contemporized dance* is contingent on now, but not free of the shackles of histories that haunt and inform the twenty-first century. Identifying as working-class, Black and female, I am reminded that the aesthetic of Western dance has marginalized bodies like mine (Gottschild, 2003). These are the very issues of presence and visibility many architects and engineers are attempting to resist designing into the cities they make.

We carry the legacy of the modernist movement where the architect is the mastermind, the maestro, we have been called many things. We go to architecture school, at least for my generation, we were told we were semi-gods, creating something new. There is a power and an entitlement which is blended in through the way of thinking when you think about designing. And I think we really need to provoke that, and challenge that sort of thinking, because that takes out the element of really listening – to a space, to a situation, to a group of people – and really designing with them . . . There are so many new paradigms of co-creation and co-designing, where I think architecture is going to.

(Architect **C. VASILIKOU,** *conversation July 2019*)

How we acknowledge the multiple bodies, histories and movements of each other must become a part of the technique, aesthetics and reflections used to create dance as much as it becomes a part of the challenge to urban design. The contingencies for what dance can be provide cultural, sociological and personal aesthetic parameters of *Place* and people that speaks to how we design spaces to live out those parameters in. As we dance together across subject or discipline boundaries it is important that we take into account our own backgrounds and histories.

Similarly, as I host movement conversations, as the choreographer in the room, it is important I do not impose 'dance' as a culture of its own onto those collaborating with me from outside of the field of dance. Dance needs to be available to become the person dancing with me, and yet also be present in the studio for that person to *step* into.

> A few people have arrived early to the sharing workshop. They nervously put the shoes they took off to come into the dance studio down in the corner, rearrange the contents of their bags, or pull out the ticket they booked to join the event. Each time someone enters I attempt to nonchalantly walk over and introduce myself, wanting them to feel welcome. At the same time hoping my greeting does not suddenly launch them into feeling they are the central focus of attention before they have had a chance to arrive in the moment of being here. Aware they are deciding if I 'look like a dancer', if I can enchant dance into manifesting in this empty studio space, I remind myself they are probably more nervous than I am. As I shake hands or touch them on the shoulder people introduce themselves as architects, or PhD students, or engineers and add 'I don't dance'. I smile and lightly mutter 'everyone can dance'.

(**A. AKINLEYE,** *reflection on workshop April 2019*)

A problem of aesthetics occurs at the fluid boundaries of dance: what is considered dance by one person is not by another. In collaborations, the notion of dance needs some kind of unifying structure from which to begin.

People can often deny dance as existing in them ('I don't dance') before they have even considered what 'them-dancing' would be. Dance is often mistaken for the social, cultural and historical baggage that accompanies it. For me, the beginning of collaboration that involves dancing is about creating places of availability to move.

Taking a starting point from the paper 'Choreographing the City: Can dance practice inform the engineering of sustainable urban environments?' (Bingham-Hall and Cosgrave, 2019), the collaborative movement workshops, performances, provocations and verbal conversations of *Choreographing the City* engaged with dance as a process for understanding and reflecting through considered moving – choreographic thinking. It was the act of *doing* that produces the knowledges we were exploring: a final aesthetic outcome was not the focus. However, the notion of 'dancing' is not neutral, people have personal expectations, cultural assumptions and social aesthetics attached to what they envisage when the word is evoked. Dance also raises philosophical questions about self-determination and social expectations: Is dance judged by the observer of the dance or the dancer themselves? In other words, is it dance because it looks like dance to an observer, or is it dance because it feels like dance to the dancer? Or is it dance because someone said it was?

My role in initiating conversations is to consider and make space for how or when people who do not normally dance feel like dancers. For the purposes of exploration together, using *contemporized dance* takes on the widest interpretation of what dance is. The word 'dance' becomes bound only by the perception of the individual doing it, rather than being the more fixed entity of traditional/classical dance.

> I wanted collaborators to have the freedom to engage with the concept of dance as their own sense of expressive movement. But if it is dance because the dancer says they are dancing where do we begin when the person entering the room starts by robbing themselves of the privilege of considering themselves dancing, murmuring 'I don't dance'. I try to offer a range of routes in . . . I refer to a 'sense of freedom in dance' some collaborators might reflect on watching a ballet, while others might find ballet restrictive but conceive of the 'freedom of dance' when thinking about Hula. I try to offer dance as a felt interaction rather than something that is 'done'. But I am aware behind this I must have some structure for interaction with dance.
>
> (**A. AKINLEYE,** *reflection on workshop April 2019*)

The structure for the term 'dance' that I am using considers dance as an *interaction* with movement, rather than a kind of movement itself. The interactions that create dance are asserted here as the combination of:[5]

- Movement as an end in itself – movement made for which the purpose is the movement itself.
- Reflective biological sensation – involves movement that is considered reflective exploration of sensation from across the nervous system.
- Multiple configurations – movement that moves from and to any possible configuration of movement.

I expand on these three below.

Movement made for which the purpose is the movement itself

Here, the end goal of dance is dance itself. For instance, although it can be beautiful to watch and freeing to play, the physical experience of football is not considered dance within this set of contingencies, because the primary end to the movement is to win by scoring goals. The movement's end intent is not the movement itself but the intent to score a goal.

Movement that is considered reflective exploration of sensation from across the nervous system

Here, if movement is so habitual, regimented or controlled that sensation across the nervous system is not available to be engaged with on a level of reflective thought, it is not dance (it is possibly exercise). Conversely, however incapacitated or physically restricted one's body may be, if sensation is interacting with reflective thought it can be dance.[6]

Also, for the observer of 'dance' there is a connection with what is observed both on a reflective level but also on an empathetic level, where movements observed vicariously resonate with sensations across the nervous system of the observer. This means that what could be considered dance to the observer could at the same time not be dance for the agent observed. Here, the beauty and physical sensation of watching the footballer moving (regardless of whether they scored a goal) can be dance for the observer – though it is not for the footballer being watched (as above).

Movement that moves from and to any possible configuration

In this case, because of the intent of movement for movement itself, dance is the opening of possibility of range of movement. Although specific styles of dance limit range of movement due to the technique required to execute the steps or because they are within an aesthetic frame, the readiness of the body for the possibility of any movement (within its own capacity) being followed by another is the *dance* within the style and technique. In other words, it is not a closed set of repetitive movement; rather dance expresses or *accomplishes itself*.

> In its purest essence, dance is the motion of neurologically and kinetically endowed body in which the purpose, meaning, or value of that motion is inherent in the motion itself . . . Dance accomplishes itself.
>
> **(NIKOLAIS AND LOUIS,** 2005, p. 6)

Therefore, I am describing dance as a set of interactions between bodily sensation, reflective thought and environment. Because *dance*, here, is defined by an interaction rather than a technical form, I see dance as being a capacity that everyone can engage with. It is their perception of the interaction that limits them, not any physical ability, since the interaction becomes *dance* at whatever 'skill' level the physical body can engage with it. One might be left asking if everyone can dance then what is the point in training to dance? Why would there be such a thing as a 'professional' dancer? By my claiming that *dance* is a kind of interaction, I suggest the following distinctions.

- A 'dancer' is anyone who can recognize the *situation* for the creation of this interaction (of dance); who can find or instigate the creation of this kind of interaction and/or uses the reflective continuity of the experiences of these interactions to inform future engagement with movement. This continuity of reflection drawn from the experience of dance begins to describe the artistry of dance. Anyone can have a moment of dance – from at a party to on a stage.
- However, the individual who focuses on preparation for the circumstances of dance by fine-tuning reflective thought and muscular body in order to play with, manipulate and generate the *interaction of dance* is the 'professional dancer'/'trained dancer'. For me, those people who spend a majority of their time engaging with the situations of dance become 'professional dancers'/'trained dancers'.
- Lastly, 'dance technique' prepares one for the *interaction of dance* and provides guidelines for the safe execution of movement along particular aesthetics.

It is important to take the time to discuss how dance manifests to underpin why I see everyone (all the collaborators) as *dancing* when we are working together. The difference between us is not dancer/non-dancer, the difference is in the experiential knowing that *doing* dance renders. I suggest that people who regularly dance develop knowledges that people who dance infrequently have not developed. In my work, I collaborate with professional dancers as assistants who bring bodily knowledges to workshop situations that support those workshop participants who do not regularly dance or for those who are 'dancing' for what feels like the first time to them.[7]

FIGURE 3 *Choreographing the City: as/at the city limits* sharing workshop (2) at The Place, London, April 2019. Photo: M. Michalowska.

'Making up dances' and 'choreography'

Dance seems to be more about facilitating situations where people feel they are given permission to dance or can belong to dance, rather than any innate inability/ability to do it. Just as anyone can 'dance' I also believe anyone has the capacity to create a group of movements (make up a dance). However, as noted above, some people spend an extended amount of time reflecting and practicing the act. This is where there is a differentiation between professional/trained/practised artists and those recreationally interested. I feel there is a distinction between what is created by someone who devotes time and reflection across their life to choreographing and someone who only encounters the act of making up a dance coincidentally. Therefore, I am distinguishing between –

what I am phrasing as – 'making-up dances' and 'choreographing'.[8] I am using the phrase 'making up a dance' to represent something anyone engaging with dance can do or is doing when they create a sequence of movement themselves. In interdisciplinary workshops, I offer processes for making up dances as part of the opening up of dance to those identifying as non-dancers (architects and engineers[9]). The process of stringing movements together involves little 'editing' other than a rearranging of the order or the direction of movements. However, regardless of this, the process of *making up a dance* transfers thinking from the verbal to the bodily. During workshops and movement conversations, collaborators create movement sequences and make up dances together to non-verbally explore ideas. When a person, who generally works within a practice outside dance, comes into the studio and is involved in 'making up a dance' they gain insight into choreographic thinking, but this does not make them a choreographer. Similarly, if a choreographer went to an architect's studio and made a drawing of a house they thought would be nice, they gain insight into the thought process behind this kind of drawing, for instance, but they have not become an architect. This distinction is important because I am suggesting the knowledges in the actions of 'choreographer' are not expressed through the aesthetic of finished performance. The knowledges are gained through the ongoing engagement with the processes of creating and dance. The nuances of 'choreo-thinking' could be lost if we mistake a product for a process.

The 'choreo-thinking' process of conversation with the bodily, the [. . .], the somatic, the expression, realization and thinking of the bodily makes dance an attractive partner to those wanting to move away from the verbal within their own disciplines. Interdisciplinary exploration involving dance is often yearning for the use of this physical literacy developed through dancing. Margaret Whitehead addresses the identification of non-verbal knowledges within dance and other movement cultures by developing the concept of *physical literacy* (Whitehead, 2010). She offers a concrete set of attributes in order to recognize the use and engagement of embodied experience to make meaning. Physical literacy is a concept drawing from Whitehead's work, as well as the work of a number of Whitehead's colleagues included in her book. Whitehead articulates a clear rejection of binaries of dualism, which she describes as having become 'embedded in the Western psyche' (Whitehead, 2010, p. 22). Whitehead sees *physical literacy* as something that can be accessed by any *body*, including the very young, very old and people at times when they are physically and mentally distressed. Rather than being a measure of elite movement ability, physical literacy sits in the development of the unique experience of the embodied being and includes our sensual understanding of the environment. It also involves the recognition and development of knowledge that is not verbalized but experienced and understood within the bodily. Physical literacy developed from dance supports the articulation and reading of the embodied.

Nevertheless, the relationship between dance and choreography is not intrinsic, although dance and choreography are linked through the somatic foregrounding of movement and bodily/empathetic sensation. Within the collaborative interdisciplinary setting of the workshops dance becomes an organizing source for enquiry across immediate analytical and practical exploration of movement. Dance engages a soma/bodily-centred focus on establishing meaningful participation in the multi-layered sensation of moving. Dance appears to be able to hold the observer, the observed and the *felt* simultaneously in view. Dance, then, is seen as a methodological principle that indicates movement informed starting points of inquiry analytically, instructionally and physically, whereas choreography is a process involving application of movement, but also editing and reflecting on the analytical and practical. Choreography explores how the soma is *felt*, but also how the somatic is organized and managed; woven into how the body is received, read and observed. The orchestration of choreography appears to happen in, on and beyond the 'body' of the agent. Choreography conducts these partnerships, coming to be associated with dance because of the way dance so easily transverses doer, environment and onlooker. Choreography draws on qualities of observer/observed/felt to create affiliations of understanding (and communication) between environment, dancer, choreographer, and audience. Therefore, consideration of the environment is an aspect of choreography. All choreography is site-specific, even Western concert dance choreography designed for the stage (Humphrey and Pollack, 1979). A presentation on a stage is site-specific because it creates the unique situation of that performance experience through the equipment, shape of stage and auditorium that is the theatre. Stages are very different from each other in terms of size, the space the audience are expected to occupy, how close walls are to the stage area, the modes and access to different types of light, how the performers and audience enter the stage area. Therefore, dance choreography is always drawing on the space/time of the particular performance of the artwork to create, the audience, the experience of the *Place* of the dance. It is this embodied exploration and creative process that opens doors to the physical literacy (Whitehead, 2010) needed for non-verbal knowledges of movement and choreographic thinking.

In the workshops, as people started to adapt, change and add to their dances they started to read, communicate and narrate non-verbal exchange, developing a physical literacy. It is this non-verbal knowing and application that leads to choreography. I have called this reflective process of choreographic thinking *choreo-thinking* (Akinleye, 2019a). In workshops, we were attempting to draw on and better understand if reflective practices through choreo-thinking could provide alternative forms of engaging with environment through dancing. For instance, as one goes beyond just making a shape with one's body to how that shape is in relationship with other bodies, the room and the viewer, an editing process of choreography starts and a somatic conversation with space also emerges. *Choreography* is different from what I am calling 'making up dances' because it involves literacy in a larger palate of materials (for instance space, movement, sound, structure and texture) and it involves an active intentional communication with [. . .]. Choreography involves intentional making of site/sight – intentional *Place*-making. Therefore, from the perspective of my practice, the process of choreography can be applied to other languages for experiencing the bodily, beyond dance.

> choreography . . . as a tool which architects intentionally use, like in the Villa Savoye, Le Corbusier, he choreographs the route through the building . . . the building is designed sort of around choreography through the building.
>
> (Architects/educators **K. TROMMER AND A. DONNELLY,** *conversation June 2019*)[10]

It is this interactive *Place*-making nature of choreographing that makes it possible to see choreography as happening in subjects beyond dance. Conversations, buildings, travel can all be choreographed. But because of the bodily nature of dance's non-verbal languages, choreography rooted in dance offers a specific set of knowledges about movement. As dance is the methodology or language, choreography is the method or composition.

FIGURE 4 Slide show of images from workshop event at The Place, London, 20 April 2019, along with images from London Bridge, 'hovering' (discussed further below, page 80) and *Re:generations* performance at The Lowey, Salford, 9 November 2019. (Hover a phone camera over QR code to be taken to link.)

Choreographic dance languages

Some choreographers express seeing dance as a non-verbal language. However, it is important to note that there is a debate in dance scholarship as to whether dance should be referred to as a language, set of languages or neither (Gottlieb, 2008; Humphrey and Pollack, 1979; LaMothe and Ebrary, 2006; Tharp and Reiter, 2006). For me, dance is to a non-verbal language as sounds are to a verbal language. Dance manifests meaning through experiences: *this curved arm means something because of my experience of curve: a somatic knowledge derived from doing and feeling in the world.* These experiences (meanings) that dance stirs can be choreographed (organized) into many languages. The act of choreographing[11] manifests the language(s) itself; choreographing adds grammar, syntax and flow to the form of dance along with other elements of environment creating language(s). However, within every language system there is something leftover, inexpressible in that language (Wittgenstein and Anscombe, 1953). This phenomenon of the excess (leftover) meaning is different in the language of different disciplines: that is, different languages are adept at expressing some parts of experience and leave out other parts of experience. What you cannot say in a language tells you something about the users of that language. As dancers, choreographers, architects, engineers, coming together in workshops we learn something about each other's crafts through the nuances of what we could not communicate readily.

> every language has a structure about which we can say nothing in this language, but there must be another language that treats the structure of the first and possesses a new structure about which we cannot say anything, except in a third language – and so forth.
>
> (**BLANCHOT,** *1993, p. 337*)

Therefore, a language attempts to communicate an experience but does not create the experience or idea itself. The experience or idea pre-exists the languages used to explain that experience. Languages are representational tools for the communication of experiences and their meaning. I see dance as physical experience with the ability to be choreographed into language(s): choreography creates dance into language(s). These become a soma-centred mode of communication that speaks through a shared corporeal empathy of experiences – seeing the curve of my arm as a soft form 'is entirely due to a series of [previous] experiences' of curved and soft manipulations (Rasmussen, 1959, p. 20). These are experiences from a bodily-centred perspective that range from sensation to complex social situations. Thus, choreographic dance offers somatically based languages to exchange or manifest ideas across disciplines. I am suggesting the leftover/inexpressible of many verbal languages is served by choreographic dance languages. It is possible, with our dualist legacy of privileging the mind over the body, part of what is leftover by verbal communications is expressed in the movement of the body. This resonates with the importance Whitehead places on developing a *physical* literacy.

The meaning leftover/inexpressible in a verbal language can be captured by metaphor and *nuance* that can become cultural characteristics or gesture within that given verbal language, but that meaning is lost to direct expression within that verbal language. I am suggesting that, throughout the workshop activity of choreographic dance, it is the leftover/inexpressible (what is brought to our attention because we cannot express it in dance) that informs the architectural and engineering thinking, just as the leftover/inexpressible of architectural and engineering languages are brought to our attention because they are manifest and given form in choreographic dance. Therefore, the workshops, as we communicated using movement and verbal languages, involved a sense of translation. This was used to notice where the structure of one practice's language could not express an experience from within that same practice, but the language of another practice could convey that experience. This was useful in terms of acknowledging what is leftover/inexpressible within the languages of our own practices (choreography, architecture, engineering). The inefficiencies of translation between our disciplines (particularly using non-verbal and verbal languages) offered the positive consequence of noticing the inexpressible. Here lives the collaboration of *Choreographing the City: as/at the city limits,* the engagement of choreographic dance language as a site/sight of knowledge and meaning-making.

At times the organizers of multi-disciplinary projects are attracted to the involvement of dancers because they hope that the somatically informed nature of dance practices will come in to *fix* things. But in this I am always aware dance has its problems also; the dance world is not a perfect world. It limits the experiences of those within it just as other practices can. Working multi-disciplinarily, I have found learning can be edified in the places where dance cannot express itself, in the places where, as a dance choreographer, we tackle a difficulty. In any practice those sites of engrained difficulty are the sites that, in collaboration, illuminate information for another language/practice. So, it is not useful for dance choreography to come into a collaboration in the vein of 'do what we do' although at times that might offer a fresh somatic-based perspective. It is also going to be in the struggle one has when choreographing, that collaborating practices will find something useful, because that might not be a struggle of expression those practices engage with, or that they even perceive as a struggle because their own language seems to express it. But when someone from one language sees a struggle of expression in another language it makes them question: 'what is that in my language and mode of thinking?' 'Why is that not a problem in my language and mode of thinking?' Therefore, where the difficulty lies is where the collaboration is richest – where the other discipline can come and support that difficulty and in doing so learn more about itself.

FIGURE 5 H. Fulleylove and M Radowska-Judd, DancingStrong Movement Lab. Rehearsal July 2019. Photo: A. Akinleye.

3 FRAMEWORK
IN CONVERSATION WITH 'THE LITERATURE'

In working together in conversation with architects and engineers, I started to notice shared theory and practices in how we envision the bodily *Being* that resides across our disciplines of dance, architecture, engineering, geography and sociology. In this segment I describe a framework for this field of *Being-in-Place* that sits across our shared belief that the bodily is central to the partnership of living together in conversation, in cities and globally as citizens. The framework of *Being-in-Place* is also offered here to underpin the assertion that we can look for and use dance and choreography movement as a starting point for exploration.

When talking about dance language above, I described the movement conversations of *Choreographing the City: as/at the city limits* as dealing with what is *leftover* or *left out* from just verbal communication. This *leftover* description of these knowledges and communications should not be misconstrued as dance merely mopping-up anything still around after a verbal conversation: as if the bodily was dealing with the deficit of what the mind could not communicate in words. Although what is not verbalizable is vast, the left-over/left-out description of what is happening can be misinterpreted as placing the bodily as non-central – a supplementary tool to the 'thinking', 'talking' mind. But what we all shared in the conversations across disciplines was an innate sense that we wanted to start with the bodily, the [. . .], as the primary place of knowledges. This noticing of bodily thinking is described as follows by dance philosophers:

> There is a thus further way in which the actual moment by moment creation of the dance may be described as my thinking in movement.

> The movement that I actually create at any moment is not a thing that I do, an action that I take, a behaviour in which I engage, but a passing moment within a dynamic process, a process that I cannot divide into beginning and ending.
>
> (**SHEETS-JOHNSTONE,** 2009, p. 34)

It is this assertion that the bodily is the sight/site of knowledge that leaves people in some fields outside of somatic inquiry and dance dubious about the possibility that we can do any more than just create a pleasing movement aesthetic together. They might ask, if what we do is non-communicable in words, then how would we bring understanding back from the bodily moment of exchange we share in the workshop? Questions of how we write about, talk about what we discovered, learnt, created with dance can leave people sceptical of exploration that has dance and choreographic languages as a central mode of communication. But as I suggest above, this comes from a focus on dance in terms of its *difference* to, and lack of, the verbal – rather than seeing dance as an experience of 'thinking' in itself.

This preoccupation with questioning *if* non-verbal modes can offer approaches to knowledge exchange is because verbal communication of an idea retrospectively dominates the experience that generated it. This dominance raises the profile of the verbal communication of the idea and overshadows the importance of the experience/knowledge that generated the idea in the first place. Within many (art) practices, including dance, the act that generates the experience that engenders the knowledge and the communication of this knowledge can be simultaneous. This does not mean that the knowledge generated is any less sophisticated than knowledges communicated verbally.

I push off my left foot to begin turning and simultaneously learn the ground is uneven beneath me. I adjust my weight by moving my hip upwards, the adjustments become a nuance to the aesthetic of the turn, I whip my head round, complete the turn and yet know so much more now about the very floor I am standing on. The experience that generated the knowledge (to turn in this particular place), the communication of the knowledge, the lift of my hip, appear as part of the same act. In this case I am suggesting the lifting of my hip is the communication of the knowledge of the uneven floor. I am suggesting the hip lift is not merely an involuntary response to catch myself from falling – it is a considered movement chosen from a specific range of possible movements in the repertoire of micro placements for ballet. My choice of movement involves the syntax of the style of the dance I am doing and 'replies' to the floor within the confines of the choreographic ballet language I am using to do the turn. Someone watching me who also has knowledge of ballet language can read my turn and attain the knowledge about the floor, as well as knowledge about my physical body and personality. This example is simplified to highlight the temporal significance of doing/knowing/communicating that tend to converge in non-verbal communication, differing from verbal languages where they can diverge. Erin Manning and Brian Massumi discuss this act of doing/thinking across their book *Thought in the Act: passages in the ecology of experience*:

> Entering the dance of attention, your perceiving converged with your moving activity, and your activity was your thinking. You entered a mode of environmental awareness in which to perceive is to enact thought, and thought is directly relational.
>
> (**MANNING AND MASSUMI,** 2014, p. 10)

I take the perspective that a focus on the 'mind' has left us with forms of intricate verbal communication that are far more theorized, articulated and statically framed than physical communication. However, this does not mean that communication stems from verbal words. John Dewey's pragmatist perspective helps develop the process of understanding dance choreography and other non-verbal communication of meaning. Dewey sees verbal language as an adornment to the *act* of communicating. He suggests communication as the drive to share and collaborate meaning across the isolation of our own immediate empiricism (Akinleye, 2012). One of the struggles of doing this can lead to verbal language but communication is not brought into existence by verbal language. Other efforts to communicate include touch, movement, even breath.

> the heart of language is not 'expression' of something antecedent, much less expression of antecedent thought. It is communication; the establishment of cooperation in an activity in which there are partners, and in which the activity of each is modified and regulated by partnership.
>
> (**DEWEY,** 1958, p. 179)

Pointing out that verbal languages are not stable but change over time, Dewey emphasizes that language is primarily for shared understanding of a situation. Moreover, verbal languages are not fixed; they adapt to the needs of the user in order to communicate ideas. The partnership of moving together when we dance in workshops provides a container for communication.[1] The partnership of communication developed from moving together thus draws on memory of movement, touch, visual drawing and verbal language to construct meaning that can then be translated into the specific of any language of communication (such as writing in this book). This is with the understanding that during any translation (from one verbal language to another verbal language included) some meaning is incidentally lost and gained. Dewey's point about the partnership of cooperation that is communication implies that there is no opposition or replacement between verbal languages and movement languages; one could not be representative of the other because they are part of the same wider process of communication. An illustration of this is that when we attempt to communicate with someone else we draw on whatever means we can in order to be understood – there are no natural discontinuations where we stop and move from word to gesture and stop again, leaving gesture behind to start to use movement. The multi-layered nature of [. . .], somatic experience denotes that the dancing body not only communicates meaning through the environment of the physicality of natural world references but also, and simultaneously, through the environment of social constructions. As we dance in the workshops our movements reference these physical, social and cultural environments beyond verbal language. Therefore, spaces we inhabit co-conspire in partnerships with us to generate meaning-making when we dance. The environments we reference and inhabit to communicate are the very spaces architects and engineers are designing.

I found that those architects and engineers collaborating in conversation with me (coming from the sense of the bodily being central) want the spaces they design to reach out and communicate with the bodily 'Beings' that move through them – to meet halfway, in multiple ways. Dancing and making up dances together – shaping the space in the room, creating rhythms of movement – seemed to affirm that environment is part of the partnership of communication. Collaborators saw dance as embodying and affirming that within their own practices it was reasonable to work from the point that environment is also in a palpable partnership of communication with those within it. In workshops, during talks and at performances we came together in dance to communicate the lived experience.

Who 'we' are

Until this point, I have been referring generally to the people in conversation with me as *architects* and *engineers*. But of course, there are many fields across this umbrella description. Just as I bring my own perspective of dance informed by my individual history and personal practice so too do the people I have been in conversation with. When asking people to describe their personal practice, each warns me that their description is atypical of their practice title. But I think this is symptomatic of the homogeny we are all attempting to challenge by engaging with interdisciplinary work. Who is to say we must find mundane similarities to understand each other, when the varieties of difference are so much more elegant in revealing the possibilities for what can be achieved within a field of practice? Therefore, the 'we' of these conversations in the field we created together includes collaborators from urban studies also identifying with sociology: their interest is people in built environments – the economics, political and transformational impact in the exchange of person in environment (Ward, White and Wilbert, 2011); and people who identify as urban designers interested in what Sowmya Parthasarasthy describes as 'the design and evolution of places, settlements and cities and how they are inhabited and re-inhabited by people and by nature'. She says, for instance,

> John Summerson's *Georgian London* (2003) is inspirational to me, the intro chapter where he describes how London grew from its two nodes, Tower of London and Westminster Palace, by filling in the gap (Strand) and moving outward, seen from a bird's eye view is pure genius! Cities are about evolution and movement. Similarly, Ian McHarg's *Design with Nature* (1969) is well before its time, the book was about environmental design and promoted a way of seeing places as layers of spatial data that helped assess what the land was 'suitable' for.
>
> *(from email correspondence with* **S. PARTHASARTHY,** *December 2019)*

We are people who are Urbanists, interested in how built environment is constituted.

> But urbanist is a strange label because if you are an urbanist you can either be studying how the build environment works or you could also be someone who is designing it. So, you can get a strange confusion between observing and making.
>
> *(Conversation with* **J. BINGHAM-HALL,** *January 2020)*

Discussion with collaborators in the area of Architectural Theory has involved analysis of design, space syntax (Hillier, 1996), thinking about networks and patterns of space, and pathways. I have spoken to people who identify as architects/educators/researchers such as Aoife Donnelly and Kristen Trommier who describe their practice as having output focuses on the generation of sensitive projects that engage with questions around the democracy of space, valuing the experience of the user. We seek solutions that resonate with cultural, historical and physical contexts, trying to simultaneously be inventive, playful, structurally/materially considered, and moving. Together, we have broad experience of public realm, arts/cultural, residential and educational projects. A reference is one that we love from Colin Ward below: 'We are groping both for a different aesthetic theory and for a different political theory. . . . The missing cultural element is the aesthetic of a variable, manipulable, malleable environment: the aesthetic of loose parts. The missing political element is the politics of participation, of user control and of self-managing, self-regulating communities'.

(from email correspondence with
A. DONNELLY, *January 2020; Ward et al., 2011, p. 132)*

Conversations have also been had with landscape architects, such as Nicole Tarrio, who see it as their work to analyse a site by looking at the existing environment and its use. To do this they consult with the local community and stakeholders in order to include as many of the community's aspirations as possible in creating a new space. Therefore, attempting to create spaces that have multifunctional purposes, in terms of use and movement – 'we like to encourage walking, seating, relaxing and promote health and wellbeing' (from email correspondence with N. Tarrio, January 2020).

I have had discussions with people working in geography exploring both the physical properties of Earth's surface and the human societies spread across it. Some geographers seek to understand where things are found, why they are there and how they develop and change over time, while some human geographers see themselves as seeking to explore the mapping of 'Selfhood' through the environment – 'how [as] "we produce space, we produce its meaning"' (McKittrick, 2006, p. xi).

I have had conversations with civil engineers who are interested in the impact of rapid urbanization, technological innovation and human wellbeing and social justice. Ellie Cosgrave suggests she is

an engineer, interdisciplinary researcher, dancer and systems thinker I am motivated by how scientific endeavour, artistic practice and policy innovation can combine to create a healthier and fairer society-particularly with respect to gender.

(from email correspondence with **E. COSGRAVE,** *December 2019)*

She offers the following quote reflecting the sociopolitical of the relationship between city and those within it.

> The right to the city is, therefore, far more than a right of individual access to the resources that the city embodies: it is a right to change ourselves by changing the city more after our heart's desire. It is, moreover, a collective rather than an individual right since changing the city inevitably depends upon the exercise of a collective power over the processes of urbanization. The freedom to make and remake ourselves and our cities is, I want to argue, one of the most precious yet most neglected of our human rights.
>
> (**HARVEY,** 2008, pp. 22–3)

Terry Roberts[2] is also a civil engineer interested in the ways in which we can take patterns, habitual ways of thinking for granted, so that they appear to 'disappear' (Fletcher, 1999).

> One way this shows up in our world is through the built environment. Surrounded by the city, with its square or rectangular buildings, its separation of spaces (and even whole districts) for particular purposes, it's easy to forget that this form of construction, this way of life, is the result of a certain set of assumptions about the way we should live, and the way we should design cities to enable that. In that sense, the city – and its design – is a political product. It is the outcome of our cultural values and the decision-making apparatus which operationalises them. My interest in this work therefore lies in its intersection with my own practice interests, and the ways in which differing approaches can generate new possibilities for change.
>
> *(from email correspondence with* **TERRY ROBERTS,** *December 2019)*

Across the individual conversations and group workshops, sharings and performances it was clear we were all attracted to the transactional nature of person-in-space and -time: the idea that environment and *Being* affect, shape, complete one another, and that this transaction is not a *neutral* exchange but is negotiated through social, physical and cultural power structures that privilege some states of environment and some bodies over others. What resonated across the discussions was the acknowledgement of the heavy responsibility of being a part of systems which often just reaffirm people's role in hierarchies rather than acknowledging people's multi-layered presence in the city.

Collaborators intuitively felt that to unpick dominant hierarchical approaches that repeatedly privilege certain small groups of citizens and environments, along with the goal to present alternative designs, the consideration of underexplored forms of composition was needed. Choreographic dance is a form of compositional approaches and strategies that have the advantage of focusing on the embodied/emplaced experience. Its movement language that traverses subject/object, by being present in dancer, dance and dancing simultaneously, its attention to creating the experience of being in a place, all offer opportunity for reconsidering how we construct living together. Dance choreography resides in the poetics of how we can exist fully (as a *Being*) in the assemblage of now (*Place*) *Being-in-Place*.

A *Being-in-Place* framework

As I was instigating the interactions of conversation, sharings and performances I worked from my own pragmatist *Being-in-Place* framework, which I share here in discussion with the literature. Collaborating in an interdisciplinary exchange, it is important for me to work from a cohesive framework that can resonate across the sense of the lived experience, our hopes and shared interests in the embodied. This is to offer my theoretical framework from a dance perspective which I call *Being-in-Place*. As a dancer and choreographer, I am coming from an embodied/emplaced perspective of connection. This involves a rejection of 'mind' and 'body' and other dualist polarities. These binaries can be replaced with blended, open spectrums. For me, the relationship of world with Self requires an openness to sensation, feeling and intuition: an openness to [. . .]. These are qualities and experiences that compel a unity between the reflections of the 'mindful' and sensations of the bodily to make meaning of the world around (Dewey, 2005; Māhina, 2002; Pratt, 2002). For me, Dewey offers the Western articulation of a framework of interaction, of embodiment, that resonates with the transaction of body and world experienced while dancing, but also addresses theoretical questions of the ontology and epistemology of the lived experience. I am suggesting pragmatism works as a lens through which to view and examine soma-centred inquiry. Pragmatism and Dewey's work particularly resonate with non-Western world views I have gained through being involved with dances from my Yoruba and Lakota backgrounds.

From my embodied perspective, I am assuming the act of living is an act of constant inquiry for learning. 'Things' are understood as contingent on the *situation* they are a part of. The body is open and connected through being in transaction, a part of world around, that creates the situation of 'now'. I use Dewey's lexicon of *situation* and *transaction* (see also Glossary and Figure i). For Dewey, *situation* can be seen as the sum of the elements that engender an experience. The elements come together through transaction. In a letter responding to Albert G. A. Balz's questions about his linguistic use of the word 'situation', Dewey writes:

> 'Situation' stands for something inclusive of a large number of diverse elements existing across wide areas of space and long periods of time, but which, nevertheless, have their own unity.
>
> (**DEWEY ET AL.,** *1989, p. 281*)

For me as a dancer, *situation* can be explained through the moment of 'nowness' that dance inhabits – the interconnection of my Self with this moment and all its past/present/future associations.

Situation

Situation can be described as the 'container' or assemblage in which the action (transaction) is happening. The container itself is made up of the elements in transaction. Therefore, if the elements change, so does the container/*situation*. Dewey gives the example of a fearful noise to demonstrate how, when 'one' perceived element of a situation changes, the whole experience changes.

> I start and am flustered by a noise heard. Empirically, that noise is fearsome; it really is, not merely phenomenally or subjectively so. That is what it is experienced as being. But, when I experience the noise as a known thing, I find it to be innocent of harm. It is tapping of a shade against the window owing to movement of the wind. The experience has changed; that is the thing experienced has changed – not that an unreality has given place to a reality, nor that some transcendental (unexperienced) reality has changed, not that truth has changed, but just and only the concrete reality experienced has changed.
>
> (**DEWEY,** *1977, p. 169*)

Dewey suggests that 'things' *are* what they do: ontologically, the 'thing' is what it is epistemologically understood as – what it is experienced as. Consider that a 'thing' is not in a subject/object relationship. In this case, noise and the person hearing it are both part of the *situation*, which creates them both (fearsome noise, fearful person). Throughout Dewey's work there is no expectation that at some point there is a singular truth of the *situation*. In Dewey's discussion of the noise–window–person–hearing–fear, these elements create and belong to the *situation* itself. For instance, fear does not belong to the noise or the person; fear belongs to the *situation, the assemblage of* noise–window–person–hearing–fear. As the *situation* changes with the new experience of knowing-window-shade-is-making -the-noise, both the noise and person hearing it ontologically change, the *situation* changes from containing fear, or fear is located differently in the *situation*. Situation is a matrix of living embodiment (that is 'mind', 'body', 'environment' = meaning-making[3]) that replaces mind (subject) and body (object) polarity (Hildebrand, 2008).

Dewey's rejection of the notion of subject/object polarities is replaced with a concept of a transactional world. This is a world that gives itself meaning through how it is interacted with. Transaction is essential in order for things to 'exist'. The world is not just exchanging 'thing' with 'thing', 'things' constitute each other through their 'transaction' with each other. In my choreography, I often use projected light which offers an analogy for transaction. The light needs the form of the dancer in order to be recognizable just as the dancer needs the light in order to be recognizable; there is a transactional relationship because as dancer and light transact their form is created. In their transaction many layers of form are also created. The dancer, people, space, light, sound, rhythm become the moment of choreography, just as the people, space, light, sound, rhythm become the moment of the city building (see Figure 4: QR link to *Re:generations* performance in film).

'Mind-ful-body' in transaction

Dewey sees no separation between epistemology (knowing) and ontology (what is to be known); for him there is no gap between subject and object.

> The reader will recall that in our general procedure of inquiry no radical separation is made between that which is observed and the observer in the way which is common in the epistemologies and in standard psychologies and psychological constructions. Instead, observer and observed are held in close organization. Nor is there any radical separation between that which is named and the naming.
> **(DEWEY, BOYDSTON AND LAVINE,** *1989, p. 96)*

Dance exemplifies this interconnectedness. The artist is both the dancer (perceiver) and the dance (perceived). As such, dancers are engaged across this through the reflective process of responding in order to dance. Dance poses physical questions, while at the same moment providing the physical answers. For instance, an arabesque[4] can be seen as the physical question: How do I stand on one leg? How do I balance on this floor in this space? How can I bend my back and remain up right? These questions are asked in the minute adjustments the dancer continually makes in order to dance the arabesque – each adjustment is the momentary solution to the question. A person who stands frozen with their leg stuck out behind them (unengaged with the physical question) is noticeably different from the dancer engaged in the 'question of arabesque'. Dance exemplifies Dewey's claim that

> ideas are statements not of what is or what has been but acts to be performed.
>
> **(DEWEY ET AL.,** 1984, p. 111)

In *Blood Memory* Martha Graham tells a story of being with Helen Keller that resonates with Dewey's statement above.

> She [Helen Keller] said to me once, in that funny voice of hers, 'Martha, what is jumping? I don't understand'.
>
> I put Merce Cunningham, then a member of my company, at the barre, and placed Helen's hands on Merce's waist. 'Merce', I said, 'be very careful. I'm putting Helen's hands on your body'.
>
> Merce jumped in the air in first position while Helen's hands stayed on his body. Everyone in the studio was focused on this event, this movement. Her hands rose and fell as Merce did. Her expression changed from curiosity to one of joy. You could see the enthusiasm rise in her face as she threw her arms in the air and exclaimed, 'How like thoughts. How like the mind it is'.
>
> **(GRAHAM,** 1991, pp. 148–9)

As well as exemplifying Dewey's 'mind' as the action of the body, dance also blurs the subject/object divide because of its use of the human body as both the vehicle and canvas for the art. Dance is both what the dancer is doing and what they are being. This gives dance choreography unique qualities of communication. The human body in dance carries with it additional meaning, as it shares empathic knowledge with the onlooker's bodily experiences. That is not to say that dance cannot be objectified[5] but that we can vicariously feel within our own body the feeling of what we are watching. This vicarious embodied understanding of form is also discussed in architecture (Pallasmaa, 2005; Rasmussen, 1959):

> when we say that such a cup has a 'soft' form, it is entirely due to a series of experiences we gather in childhood, which taught us how soft and hard materials respond to manipulation. . . . And this conception of soft and hard forms, acquired from objects small enough to handle, is applied even to the large structures.
>
> (**RASMUSSEN,** *1959, p. 20*)

The shared sensation of humanity is experienced through having a human body. This means that the bodily (movement, touch, breath and so on) has meaning to people beyond a theoretical understanding. Movement tells a *story* as it is empathically understood it is as if it is *read*. Embodied beings communicate with each other by referencing their own embodied experiences by referencing their knowledge of [. . .]. In *Martha Graham: A Dancer's Life*, Graham's biographer Russell Freedman recounts the following about her:

> She was a little girl. She stood looking up at her father, her hands clasped tightly before her, her cheeks burning with shame and humiliation.
> 'Martha', said her father, 'you're not telling me the truth, are you?'
> Martha's lips trembled. Tears welled in her eyes.
> Kneeling down, her father put an arm around her. 'Don't you know when you do something like this, I always know? There is always some movement that tells me you are deceiving me . . .' It was as though her body had spoken. Looking back many years later, she [Martha] said, 'that was my very first lesson as a dancer'.
>
> (**FREEDMAN,** *1998, p. 15*)

This is not to suggest that the body 'gives us away' or betrays some inner truth even when we want to hide it. The example from Graham is about the language of movement and how it is a commonly used form of communication that is understood vicariously. As we grow from child to adult, we can learn to lie with our bodies as much as with our words (and our spaces), but nonetheless, 'lies' or 'truth', the bodily is in mindful communication beyond itself.

There is an ambiguity in what dance is; where it is. Dancers have expressed that dance is both the dancer's body and the movement in space; that the dance resides in the relationship of body, intent and space. This resonates with Dewey's notion of *Transaction* and his matrix of mind-body-environment (embodiment): the dance is present in the dynamic of dancers' bodies in space. However, as with *Transaction*, one cannot separate the elements; instead, they qualify each other (see Figure i).

> We know that sensation occurs as a response to change in the body or environment. The senses register differences in degrees, which, in essence, are dynamics. The artist's skill in perceiving and in responding are two of his primary functions and should be practiced daily in class through total sensory involvement.
>
> **(NIKOLAIS AND LOUIS,** 2005, p. 28)

Dance choreographers Alwin Nikolais and Murray Louis begin to describe the experience of dancing as a response to what, in the Deweyan lexicon, could be described as the *immediate empiricism* of a *situation*. In *A Widening Field*, dancer Miranda Tufnell and architect and sculptor Chris Crickmay also offer a notion of this. As with Nikolais and Louis, Tufnell and Crickmay highlight the importance of 'being present' in the bodily, 'arriving into the body, into the world'.

> certain details in what is around me or in my sensing body begin to call out to my attention . . . These are moments when our sensing comes into connection with the wider field of who and where we are, and we seem to move out of ourselves – we begin to imaginatively participate in the world around us.
>
> **(TUFNELL AND CRICKMAY,** 2004, p. 32)

Dewey believes that sensitivity and awareness in experiences would allow people to have fully engaged lives as members of society;[6] to *imaginatively participate*.

The activity of dancing appears to shed more light on the interplay of *aesthetic and intellectual* experience, which, according to Dewey, happen in the body with the mind being the action of them. Reflective thought is the action of the 'mind–full–body' (Dewey, 1958, 1997, 2005, 2007; Dewey et al., 1984). Although his goal was not to describe dance per se, Dewey captures Martha Graham's 'unity' of the movement of dance (Graham in Morgan, 1980, p. 11). In his description of an experience, Dewey unites all the elements of a *situation*, that is the connection between space danced in, dancer's body and intent. For Dewey, an experience contains not just *what* is experienced but also *how* it is experienced: the 'body' – organs, muscles – feel *what* is happening, but also the consciousness of a narrative or recognition of feelings of the experience itself informs how it is experienced (see Figure i).

The 'mind' is the action of the 'body'. Dewey explains this in *Art as Experience* when he presents the mind as a verb, a thread through the activity of being.

> It [dualism] has treated mind as an independent entity which attends, purposes, cares, notices, and remembers. This change of ways of responding to the environment into an entity from which actions proceed is unfortunate, because it removes mind from necessary connection with the objects and events, past, present and future, of the environment with which responsive activities are inherently connected. Mind that bears only an accidental relation to the environment occupies a similar relation to the body
>
> (**DEWEY**, 2005, p. 275)

Therefore, Dewey suggests the mind is the activity of the realizing the catalyst of feeling that embodiment engenders.

> The world we have experienced becomes an integral part of the self that acts and is acted upon in further experience.
>
> (**DEWEY**, 2005, p. 108)

Embodiment

As a choreographer, I find Dewey's writing captures 'the dialogue of feeling' that I am aware of while I move – that is what I call dance. I feel Dewey's work constructs an orientation towards a perception of the lived world that allows us to reconsider analytical and theoretical (dance) questions while still having a starting point in movement.

Although embodiment is a small area in Western philosophy, connectedness-with-world-around, which I am attributing to the nature of embodiment, is a shared value across many Indigenous and Africanist world views throughout the globe, predating Western dualist systems of colonialism (such as Allen, 1992, regarding Native American and feminist recovering of intraconnection with world around). Many Africanist and Indigenous world views have side-stepped dualist divides of mind and body, even when colonialism attempted to enforce them. Scott L. Pratt argues that Dewey's (and other pragmatists') distinctiveness in European philosophy at the time they emerged in the late 1800s is in part due to it being grounded in the Native philosophy of America of which Dewey, living and working in America, would have experienced. In *Native Pragmatism* (2002), Pratt presents evidence and documentation of Native American philosophy before European contact and during the beginning of European occupation. He notes particularly the Northeastern Native Culture concept of 'wunnegin'[7] along with a symbiotic approach to relationships with the environment as informing Dewey's pragmatist ideas of pluralism, community and transaction. The impact of Northern American Indigenous world views is often invisiblized by the colonial history and the expansionist principles of the United States. Indigenous attitudes to the environment clashed significantly with the Europeans who began to populate/occupy America. Indigenous American philosophy did not relate to the environment as something to own but instead saw the land as something that indicated how it should be lived *with* (Black and Neihardt, 1932). This philosophy can be understood through the notion of *situation*: one would not own the *situation*; one is a part of it. In the paper 'The Given Land: Black Hawk's conception of place', Pratt (2001) argues that Native peoples located/locate themselves in terms of their environment rather than in terms of an external time.

> The European or dominant approach to meaning is characterized by an interest in unification, universals, and certainty. The [Indigenous] American approach, rather than being a simple negation of the dominant approach, is a genuine alternative, focusing interest on interaction, particularity, and pluralism. At the center of this alternative is an approach to meaning grounded in what can be called a 'logic' of place. Despite its status outside the mainstream, this indigenous American approach has nevertheless dramatically affected the course of European American thought and history through its influence on American feminism, African American thought, and even on classical American philosophy.
>
> (**PRATT,** 2001, p. 109)

Pratt cites events where Native American nations saw one's own actions as being formed by one's environment. The *Logic of Place* is a notion conceived by Pratt in order to denote the idea that the environment indicates how it is engaged with. *Logic of Place* highlights the role of identity in transaction. *Place* indicates how it can be interacted with. Pratt refers to the autobiography of Black Hawk (1990) to demonstrate the importance of *Place* in the construction of identity in general. This is an idea that means the *Place* that shapes you appears in you as much as you appear in it. Pratt reminds us that when (it is reported) Indigenous nations said of white people, 'they should go back to their own lands', this was not a statement of ownership of land (which is not an Indigenous concept); it was an assumption that the misaligned, alien activities of the white people must have been crafted in their relation to a place that was different from 'this one' since it did not fit with 'this one'. Therefore, they must seek the place it matched in order to live harmoniously. As white people adapted the land and the land adapted them, they started to appear to fit more. Black Hawk notes this as the Appalachian Mountain people appeared to fit with the land more when he visited the area after it had been occupied for a number of years (Pratt, 2001).

Pratt largely focuses on the implications of understanding oneself and others in spatial terms. The *Logic of Place* demonstrates the transactional awareness of being in the natural world. The *Logic of Place* reverberates across the notions of transaction and interaction. It also seems clear that there is an argument that one's environment contributes to one's construction of self-identity and sense of self (see Figure i).

> Rather than organizing one's self-understanding and relations with others temporally (and in the context of a kind of universal time), I proposed that American Indian traditions suggest that meaning can be organized spatially. This, of course, does not rule out sequences of events, but rather holds that their meaning is a matter of the 'spatial' relations that are instantiated in the sequences.
>
> *(from personal email correspondence from* **S. PRATT,** *May 2011)*

The *Logic of Place* suggests that the environment affects the individual's construction of Self. This is an idea also explored in phenomenology. Merleau-Ponty[8] captures the notion that one's interaction with the environment constructs oneself. For him, this interaction is more than a reaction to surroundings.

> The many tourists who are brought to the church on sight-seeing tour hardly notice the unique character of the surroundings . . . [Boys] also utilized the [church] wall in the game [of football] – a curved wall, which they played against with great virtuosity . . . I do not claim that Italian youngsters learnt more about architecture than the tourist did. But quite unconsciously they experienced certain basic elements of architecture: the horizontal planes and the vertical walls above the slopes. And they learned to play on these elements.
>
> (**RASMUSSEN,** *1959, pp. 16–17*)

> It is not enough to see architecture; you must experience it. . . . You must dwell in the rooms, feel how they close about you, observe how you are naturally led from one to the other.
>
> (**RASMUSSEN,** *1959, p. 33*)

Rasmussen suggests that people who share similar environments develop similar personality traits through their shared experiences. These form personal identities and contribute to cultural identities.

> People who live in the same country at the same time often have the same sense of rhythm. They move in the same way, they receive pleasure from the same experiences.
>
> (**RASMUSSEN,** 1959, p. 135)

Henri Lefebvre also looks at the notion of rhythm that unites people in an experience of place. In *Elements of Rhythmanalysis* (2004) Lefebvre establishes that both people and places have rhythms which constitute their route of accessibility for engagement, as well as reflecting how they have been engaged with. Geographic and cultural locations (such as Mediterranean cities) have uniting rhythms that are instrumental in the experience of how they are lived in. From my embodied perspective in dance the flow (Rasmussen), logic (Pratt) or rhythm (Lefebvre) is one of the most highly accessible elements of the assemblage of being present because the consequences of being juxtaposed to it or the sensation of being in harmony with it are deeply physical sensations – they are recognizable corporeal experiences.

The idea that environment is made distinctive through our transaction with it returns us to the interconnected construct of Dewey's *situation*. In this embodied starting point of situation, things exist in interaction, elements of situation do not exist alone. Dance does not exist alone, it comes into being in the *situation* of the transaction between body, music, intention, floor and so on. As a part of a situation 'spaces' are also subject to interaction. From an embodied perspective, space must be qualified by the event or experience that marks it as the *thing* you are talking about. To indicate this understanding, some scholars suggest the use of the word 'place' rather than 'space'. This is to indicate space is merely a mode of measure, whereas Place involves the transaction of experiencing – *Place* acknowledges it is part of the *situation*. These distinctions between *Place* and space are proposed by Casey:

> the experience of perceiving ... requires a corporeal subject who lives *in* a place *through* perception. ... Thus place integrates with body as much as body with place.
>
> (**CASEY,** 2009, p. 325)

Echoing Dewey's notion of the transaction of *situation*, Massey describes place as the coming together of processes. Here Dewey's 'situation' is described by Massey as a 'constellation of processes'.

> This is the event of place in part in the simple sense of coming together of the previously unrelated, a constellation of processes rather than a thing. This is place as open and as internally multiple.
>
> (**MASSEY,** 2005, p. 141)

Similarly, Sarah Pink draws on Howes to discuss the interrelationship between body–mind–environment, and the significance of movement (Ingold, 2000) as the manifestation of interrelationships. Pink suggests that deeper reflection on embodiment moves us away from a body-in-space towards Place – 'emplacement' (Pink, 2011).

This emplaced, *Being-in-Place* framework suggests that we exist through our interactions. We are affected by and have an effect on that which is around us. Environment is a part of who we are – our identity – because it is shaping us, as we shape it. There is a reverberation throughout postmodern thinking on 'identity' that similarly challenges the terms for, and boundaries of, the individual. Post-structuralists such as Butler (1990), Foucault (Dreyfus, Rabinow and Foucault, 1983; Foucault, Bertani, Fontana, Ewald and Macey, 2003) and Barthes (1981) challenge us to question the meaning attributed to the terms with which an individual is defined and remembered. Pragmatism defines the 'Self' as coming into being through somatic interaction with environment: embodiment, a state that is ever-changing. Permanence and certainty are also challenged through concepts that *knowing* is not solely a function of the conscious brain but a part of the ever-changing rhythms of transaction. This has been made tangible for me to notice/understand through dancing choreography.

> A shadowless sensation, that opens the muscles of my back as the weight in my arms succumb to the walls sliding me slowly down to where the spongy linoleum of the dance floor welcomed the percussion of my knee, and then thigh, and then hip. Legs folded out into the space of the room, ribs opened into concrete, side of my head caressed against the wall, sitting curve-like into corner of wall-floor, I sighed into the position we – wall, floor, breath, and bone – temporarily made of my Self.
>
> (**A. AKINLEYE,** *reflection 2. From rehearsal of . . . Whispers. Choreographer Helen Kindred, 4 November 2019*)

Identity through the somatic experience of *Being-in-Place*

Dance in conversation with architecture and engineering can arrive at a shared sense of a thing's identity being established through transaction between the *Being* of (living things) and event of *Place* (the constellation of processes that are the moment). In conversation with architects and engineers, we shared an interest in the processes of the *situation* of *Being-*

in-Place. Integral to this is the belief that the bodily reaches out and meets the environment and environment reaches out and meets the body. Our consciousness and identity linger at the moment where they meet (see Figure i). But this beautiful sense of co-creation is often simplified in order to discuss it and recognize feeling it. The lived-experienced of the transactional reality of life involves complex layers of social and cultural history and expectation: complicated by how we learn to identify the edges of a perception of Self in the matrix of body–mind–environment and how others identify us there. Massey (2005) also suggests that space is produced rather than inert.

Self as in transaction is additionally layered by how/where/when one experiences the blur with one's environment: where consciousness of Self manifests in the body–mind–environment matrix. This is given a further interesting perspective by Deleuze and Guattari (Deleuze and Guattari, 1983, 1987; Dunbar, 2004). Deleuze and Guattari pose the question of where the body ends or begins. They see each organ as having a consciousness of which the 'conscious' brain may not always be aware. The body is no longer made real by the perception of the brain.[9] The body is a knowledgeable entity (machine) as it communicates across itself and 'outside' of itself. The edges of this body (machine) can be added to and extended with eyeglasses, computer keyboards, wheelchairs, prosthetic limbs, etc. Deleuze and Guattari's 'body as machine' (and 'body without organs') resonates with descriptions dancers have made of the experience of dance, where the body is an extension into the 'elements' around. Deleuze and Guattari's 'machines' (bodies, buildings, books, 'things') are made of organic and inorganic material (Deleuze and Guattari, 1983, 1987). Thus, the edges of identity are not locked behind the skin of the individual but come into Being at the interactions of the body machine (the body without organs – beyond the skin). The impact the environment has on who people feel they are or can be is highlighted here. As experiences with environments shape the person, identity is formed across both persona and environment.

> A building is a machine [like a Deleuze and Guattarri body, having organic and in organic elements]. . . . When I encounter a building, it produces in me certain affects – lines of flight, deterritorializations, whatever. Precisely what affects it produces in me will depend on what I bring to it as part of me – my experience, ideas that I have picked up from reading, stray images that the building calls to mind . . . the building might produce in me powerful affects that are a real part of my response – my pulse rate might quicken
>
> (**BALLANTYNE,** *2007, pp. 41–2*)

Environment shaping, affecting, and being shaped by the bodily also resonates with the *connected* experience of dancing. For instance, the experience of dance contact improvisation has also been described as a collaborative shaping process of awareness/discovery giving the moment an identity.

> The world that I and other dancers are together exploring is inseparable from the world we are together creating.
>
> (**SHEETS-JOHNSTONE,** *2009, p. 32*)

The concept of bodies and environment being transactional eludes to the relationship of organic beings and non-organic environments co-creating through the grounding of being physically present. One of the major points in my conversations with architects and engineers has been to notice how identity (both of people and buildings) is shaped by that interaction. There is a layer of complication here, as the design itself is created within the premise that urban design must accommodate a sense of foretelling the identities that will interact with it. The design – blueprints of a building for instance – anticipates interactions that have not happened. The design attempts to know and facilitate interaction before it is experienced. Therefore, the complexity of the immediate empirical transactional experience of the building includes elements that predict transactions of person-with-building through the identity of the architect/engineer, who has designed a reflective proposal into the building but who is no longer present through their organic body. The building has become their body without organs, they are present in their projected anticipation of who and what will encounter the building. The architect or engineer's view on life and what is available to connect with are present in the constructed shape and projected use of the building but their felt, somatic experience of the 'made', erected building is not.

Buildings demonstrate characteristics physically etched into their structures by the architect or accommodated for by the engineer. Bodies arrive at the moment of interaction with building shaped by past experiences such as through their posture that emerges from the habit of their meaning-making. Buildings and bodies draw on socially and culturally prescribed pathways established across the past, present and anticipated future as they encounter each other. Although grounded in the physicality of being present, neither building nor human bodies are passive in production of the moment of interaction. As such both buildings and bodies are more than aesthetic lumps, they are not neutral. They are engaged and readable through drawing on physical logistics interpreted through social, cultural and historical habits of clarification. Thus, the *situation* should not be oversimplified in the theoretical mapping of *Being-in-Place* described above. *Situation* is multi-layered; situation includes cultural, social and emotional meaning-making and includes layers of sensation to the physicality of *Being* in the moment.

A critique of the phenomenological and/or pragmatist environment bodily connection is that there is a Western interpretation of an assumed 'sameness' across the experience of being present in Place (Weate, in Bernasconi, 2001). Dewey demonstrates how cultural or social interpretation impacts on the *situation* of the 'truth' of the fearful noise to window shade knocked by the wind, discussed earlier (Dewey, 1997, p. 169). But of course, Dewey has purposely simplified the description experience, knowing within that *situation* there is a harmony of multiple transactional identities. Nonetheless, the oppositional identities of fearful person/not fearful person are sequential. During the fearful noise incident, Dewey's man has some agency or freedom over his identities of fearful-man to man-looking-at-window-shade. This is not least because there is a sense of a temporal progression where the man has time to register a fearful noise and then time to experience 'closer examination', followed by time to move into the situation of 'window shade being knocked by the wind'. In *Black Skin, White Masks*, Frantz Fanon (2008) points to situations where oppositional identities are not sequential but simultaneous. Fanon describes sitting on a train in 1930s Europe, present in the transactional physical identity of a man on soft train seat, in the warmth of a carriage – the past/present/anticipated future of being 'a man among men', a man-going-to-work, perhaps. Then a white child says 'Look, a Negro, I am frightened'. This statement propels Fanon into a *Place* that includes being the white child's perception of frightening Blackness.

> 'Look, a Negro! Mama, a Negro!'
>
> 'Shh! You'll make him angry [to child]. Don't pay attention to him, monsieur, he doesn't realize you're just as civilized as we are [to Man].'
>
> My body was returned to me spread-eagled, disjointed, redone, draped in mourning on this white winter's day. The Negro is an animal, the Negro is bad, the Negro is wicked, the Negro is ugly; look, a Negro; the Negro is trembling.
>
> (**FANON,** 2008, p. 93)

DuBois (1989) suggests a *double consciousness* is needed in order to respond to this experience of opposing identities happening simultaneously. The complication of Dewey's 'window blind situation' is that to understand

Dewey's point about transaction we willingly objectify 'frightening noise' and 'window shade'. We slip into understanding the flexibility of the 'truth' of the *situation* by adopting a sense of subject (man), object (noise) or object (window shade). Fanon reminds us that certain identities and their physical attributes have been objectified (such as Negro). Looking at the situation of the frightening noise/window shape from the perspective of the cloth and plastic of 'the-thing-at-the-window' (which has been both 'frightening noise' and 'window shade') we are happy to assume its essence can be understood contingent upon the subject's perception of it – we are happy to consider it is placid. As an object its essence is changeable in the transaction through the perception of the subject (man). But women, wheelchair users and 'Negros', as Fanon points out, have been objectified, therefore complicating *situation* beyond just a peaceful co-creation of reality. For that and for those who are objectified, their essence is responded to through the perception of those who perceive themselves as 'subject' and outside of what they are perceiving. Part of the *situation* of *Being-in-Place* is that cultural and social constructs add layers to *situation* that can rob some people of the freshness and responsiveness of *now* and expect them to be culpable for histories and expectations established elsewhere. To weigh down the potential of nowness with expectational limits is one of the crimes of prejudice, of course. Identifying myself (and with the physical attributes that read) as a Black, working-class woman living across European–American settings, I experience the complications that require DuBois's double consciousness as a strategy to organize interaction. My female body, brown skin and working class-isms are often objectified. The transaction of *situation* very often includes historical and social expectations of what I am as part of the attributes of the moment I find myself a part of. These experiences confirm for me that the *lived experience* of transaction is not a neutral state.

Firstly, neutrality is vanquished in the constructs of Being and *Place*, by the presence of notions of ownership. Attitudes towards ownership are implicit: the land (on which the city is built) has been seen as an object to be owned. European colonial attitudes of expansionism justified laws giving permission to address land as object to capture, own and build on (Trask, 1993). Similarly, women's bodies have been and are objects to be owned, as Black bodies have been objects to be owned. European legislation has supported treating women's bodies as objects to be captured, owned and reproduced with, and non-white bodies have been used as objects to be captured, owned and built with (Anderson, 2000; Butler, 1990; DuBois, 1989; McKittrick, 2006; Thompson, 2014). Therefore, notions of land, property, Blackness and femininity share social and cultural narratives that span across the transaction of environment/person. They have all been commodified as elements (of environment) that have closed and limited perimeters for what they mean or can contribute to the moment. The lived transactional experience is weighted by these histories' projection into *now* and future, even as we feel the interconnection of Self and world around that dance offers insight into.

Secondly, there is a danger from relying on a sense of *norm*. This gives sanction to a standardized anticipation of what to expect from people and building. Western urban designs can be seen as not passive in the construction of the types of identities that are most accessible when within the buildings they construct. Therefore, if the 'norm' of white, tall, male is the most indicated identity for physical engagement with a building, my presenting as small, Black, female comes into tension with the designed area (how do I 'dance' with this?). On entering a building, the liberty to be the norm in my own narrative and meaning-making is less available to me than the tall, white man who enters the same building. Therefore, the interactive bodies of wheelchair user or Black-ness, or female, or older, or working-class, or child all bring with them micro-layers of difficulty in terms of the ability to have a consistency of self-identity that is not dominated by a *norm* unavailable to them physically, yet designed into the urban spaces they are in transaction with.

My *Being-in-Place* framework suggests that the world is multi-layered – a polyrhythmic constellation of processes. As we (dancers, choreographers, architects, engineers) came together in dance and verbal discussion, across disciplines, the uniting element between us was a shared sense of a world that is interconnected and a shared interest in addressing the potential joys, and potential injustices, the interconnection of the city world manifests. For me, this is a drawing together of my lived experiences of dancing where the transaction of my muscles, bones, music, breath, floor, other dancers, walls, histories interconnecting, creating each other. This seems to demonstrate Dewey's description of a transactional interrelated lived experience, as well as echoing many Africanist and Indigenous world views such as Lakota philosophy of *Mitakuye Oyasin*, translated as 'we are all connected/we are all related'. This is where the movement and verbal conversations started.

PART TWO

In Part One, I explored interconnectedness and transaction as apparatus for understanding *Being*. I have also suggested the notion of *Place* as a shared significance across the practices of choreography, architecture and engineering. My hope is that the *Being-in-Place* framework I offer in Part One scaffolds the exploration and reflections in the subsequent sections of Part Two and Part Three.

Now, in Part Two, I explore two shared emerging themes from the workshops, rehearsals, performances and verbal conversations that arose during *Choreographing the City: as/at the city limits* in 2019 and 2020. Therefore, nuanced by the interconnected paradigm of *Being-in-Place*, Part Two is made up of collections of essays, poems, choreography and dialogue drawn together under two themes: *Chasing Stillness* and *Lingering in Dwelling/Residing in Wandering*. The first section of Part Two comprises essays, poems, choreography and verbal conversations that led to the theme of *Chasing Stillness*, followed by a section of essays, poems, choreography and verbal conversation leading to the theme *Lingering in Dwelling/Residing in Wandering*.

4 CHASING STILLNESS

Reflecting back on performances and the verbal and movement, conversations, the theme of *Chasing Stillness* emerges. This theme highlights the problem that there are parts of the city where the only kind of *relationship* one can have is the one carved out by the dominate *rhythm* of the design of the space. Rather than stillness being constituted by a lack of movement, the theme of *Chasing Stillness* reveals attention to strategies for conjuring and listening to the faint melody of new, less acknowledged relationships within *Place*. Stillness becomes about finding other possible relationships with the city beyond the thunderous drive of the dominant rhythm white-straight-male-employed.

FIGURE 6 A. Akinleye and H. Fulleylove dancing on London Bridge, October 2019. Photo: A. Califano.

Citybody

Eric and I are sitting in a glass room in an international architectural firm. Two sides of glass look out over London and one wall of glass looks into an open plan office area with many people busy at work. The last wall is solid brick, holds a white board and divides this meeting room from the next meeting room. There is a round table between us. Eric is a civil engineer. As we wait for two of Eric's colleagues to join us, I ask Eric what it means to be a civil engineer. He explains his field by using the body as a metaphor for the elements of his work. The body is the city, the people are the blood. He sees his job as civil engineer to help get the blood (people) around the body (city). I ask if the buildings could be organs in Eric's 'Citybody' metaphor and he agrees. Eric says his work as an engineer is about the health of the *Citybody*. He says it divides into three elements, infrastructure, buildings and utilities. As we talk, we start to build the *Citybody*:

- Infrastructure, roads and rail are the blood vessels (people vessels); bridges and canals are connective tissue and ligaments and tendons.
- Buildings, for manufacture, health and education are where the blood (people) gather things, drop things off; buildings are like the organs and muscles.
- Utilities: gas, electrical, water systems and environmental landscapes are the nervous system of the body.

I compare these metaphors of *Citybody* to my own dancing body: my body's infrastructure of blood vessels, tendons and connective tissues as *Citybody*'s rail, canals and bridges: I remember tearing my Achilles tendon and the impact that had on movement across my whole body. I imagine the dank, rust of the railway bridge, a tendon, across the main road at my local station and think about the warning sign there that says if you see any problem or accident associated with the structure of the bridge you have to report it immediately. When I have torn connective tissue – such as when I tore my Achilles – I had to 'report it'/get treatment immediately too!

I contemplate my body's nervous system as the *Citybody*'s utilities. The metaphor seems to make sense: I have acupuncture regularly to address my nervous system. In my body, years of tension in my shoulders can impact the way I breathe which impacts the amount of blood that gets to my thighs as I begin a jump. This is similar to when the electricity isn't working in one area (the traffic lights are down, the rail signals stop working properly) and less people (blood) travel across to the buildings (organs) to do their job keeping the *Citybody* moving. My acupuncture visits address the flow around my body.

I realize I am thinking, and we are talking, about body as if it were separated from mind. I ask myself if Eric's *Citybody* has a reflective mind (as the *Being-in-Place* framework assumes). Like Deleuze and Guattari's 'body as machine' (Deleuze and Guattari, 1983, 1987; Dunbar, 2004), the different parts of *Citybody* would be communicating independently in different networks of consciousness (building to building). This thought makes Deleuze and Guattari's 'body as machine' metaphor really clear; of course, in *Citybody* there are main throughways of communication that give *Citybody* a kind of personality that directly affects how that city interacts with other cities, but there are also transactions below the 'radar' (building-organs communicating with each other independently).

I contemplate the *Citybody* in terms of Dewey's mind-ful-body. I run through the metaphor considering what the 'mindfulness' of the *Citybody* would be: something that moves the *Citybody* into reflective action. If 'body' is 'city', then mind-fulness could be the money, legislation and building codes that shape people's access to the buildings of the city. Money, legislation and building codes would act as the instigator of reflective action that shapes *Citybody*'s activity.

Knowing most people do not consciously come from my dancer perspective of embodiment, I ask Eric and Larry, another civil engineer who has joined us now, 'Where is the mind in the city?' I am aware that mind and brain are often interchangeable when people talk about the body more generally. The question could be answered as we have done in the West for hundreds of years, by suggesting the mind is in the brain and the brain is one of the bigger more impactful organs (buildings). Thus, the *Citybody*'s mind would be in a building associated with legislation or money, for instance the parliament building or police station of a city or central bank. Then Deleuze and Guattari's 'body as machine' could still apply: each organ as having a consciousness of activity of which the 'conscious' brain (parliament building/central bank) is not always aware.

But Larry says he thinks that information technology is starting to be the 'mind' of the city. He points to cities like Hangzhou, China, where information for the city has been centralized. The *City Brain* project (Beall, 2018) has been storing data generated across a city in a cloud-based system. This is then used by Artificial Intelligence to inform the control of the city. I can see how this still fits our metaphor: the *Citybody*'s reasoning mind is why people (blood) would move from building (organ) to building (organ) to create activity. It could be suggested that people move from place to place based on the *reasoning* of the online information they get about weather, train schedules, what time it is in general, if there is a sale or even what road (blood vessel) is working best. As all of this is brought to them through information technology, Larry suggests that as IT starts to gather data in the Cloud and begins increasingly distributing it to the people there will be less need to travel. Larry says, 'This will change Urban Design. People can work from home, know not to go out if there is congestion on the roads'. I think the *Citybody* is working towards being more static, but Eric and Larry optimistically see this as an opportunity for *Citybody* to have more activity to do with pleasure than work: 'work from home then go out to walk in the park,' says Eric.

I think about how ironic it is that there is a future for *Citybody* that takes the mind out of body and into a nebulous cloud in the same way that Cartesian dualist moved to separate esoteric mind from physical body in Western philosophy 400 years ago: a separation of mind and body in Cartesian terms where body merely responds and is controlled by mind. I wonder if this means we are working towards disembodied cities.

When I get home after Eric, Larry and I have spoken together, I consider Dewey's matrix of mindful body–environment and realize our *Citybody* metaphor is environment-less. We were talking about the city as if it was a closed complete system of mind and body. Using our metaphor, I wonder if environment would be the history, social discourses and attitudes around *Citybody*.

Many civil engineers I have spoken to are very concerned with the quality of individuals' lives and, at times, they feel general practices of engineering do not support them in this. In the *Citybody* metaphor civil engineers are working to keep the body *moving*. Meanwhile the *mind* seems to be moving out of the body (for instance to the Cloud). While the *environment* of histories and social discourses that impact *Citybody* are often ignored as part of the process, engineers are tasked with keeping the body moving regardless. But it seems *Citybody* is a disembodied entity that forces them to focus on functional repair. To this end, safety is instilled in engineering training. But in the displaced, disembodied *Citybody*, engineers suggest they are mostly working with a safety that is limited to a closed focus on making sure blood (people) remains moving around the *Citybody*, regardless of the characteristics of the blood cells being moved. In other words, as long as blood (people) arrives at and lives in organs (buildings) safely, the job is done. Blood (people) is homogenized in order to keep moving. Questions about the diversity of the blood (people) are overshadowed by the importance of them just being there. So, as engineer Ellie Cosgrave points out (when I discuss this with her), there is little attention for how some blood cells (people) remain rich and full, while others remain undernourished as they travel around *Citybody*. And those who do not or cannot be homogenized drop out of the action of the city – disappear.

It seems there is more room for an emplaced *Citybody* at the design phase of a project as architects, urban designers and landscape designers draw on histories of areas, attempt to challenge social constructs and look at aesthetics. At this beginning point they can emplace the city but when it gets to the engineers the main question they must address is 'does the *Citybody* work? Are the blood vessels, tendons and organs safe[1] and working, is there a pulse – are we moving?'

A conversation on waiting

In the role of choreographer collaborating with architects and engineers I had thought that moving and movement would be what I would directly bring to the conversation, but as I was introduced to different projects and processes I felt there was an abundance of knowledge about movement already in the practices of the people collaborating with me.[2] As with the concern for *Citybody*'s flow of movement around it, keeping moving seemed as if it was the imperative of many of the designs I looked at. The designs attended to how people will enter, where they will pause (their dwell time) and how they will exit. I noticed that all the designs shared with me and conversations about them were about moving. So, I asked about stillness in a conversation with Eric, civil engineer, and colleague Terry, technical director, involved in bidding for large public sector projects.

Adesola: I have been really interested in the part of the design that designers call 'dwell time'. Planning for dwell time areas seems as if it is not really about stopping, because when you design, dwell time is within the journey of the design. So, dwelling then becomes part of movement, really – part of the journey. These dwell time pauses could be thought of as just like slowed down movement. But I cannot perceive them as sped-up stillness which makes we wonder about what stillness is in urban design.

> **Eric:** Dwelling as slowed down movement . . . I think that seems quite logical. If you enter a space, and then you don't go into a 'destination' – like an office – you are there in a

transitory position. So, whether it be to catch your breath before you go and embark upon the next part of your travel, to kill time before you catch a train, that dwelling is part of an ongoing journey. I suppose it all depends where you draw the line as to how long you need to be somewhere for it not to be dwelling. Are we dwelling whilst we sit here? Because I almost view my day as like a circular journey – from home to here [the office] to home. That's not because I'm always looking forward to five o'clock and getting home again [!!], but my thought is always that it's a complete loop. So, I am now dwelling really, because I'm not travelling anywhere.

Terry: Yes, it's quite an interesting way to come at it. Because it makes me realize how rarely I am static in a city. If I am static, I'm usually treating it as waiting. It's not a good thing for me to be static in the city; it's because 'Oh, I'm due somewhere at three o'clock and I'm running half an hour early, so I'll have a cup of coffee.' I didn't mean to be still, I just find myself unexpectedly not moving.

Adesola: I was recently asked to contribute to a project about what artists do to prepare to work.[3] After a long conversation, we concluded that a lot of things that you do before you start work is sort of waiting, waiting for inspiration to come, and that generally people think of waiting as a kind of negative thing, but it's part of the process of doing. In a way, artists account for waiting (make space for it) in their process. And I wonder if is 'waiting' is ever a part of a design.

Terry: I don't think it is.

Eric: A lot of design almost falls down to a cost/benefit analysis. You are going to spend money on designing and building something and it's to generate some sort of commercial benefit out the other end, so if you can save on journey times, if you can reduce accidents, it all has a benefit to the economy. So, having an *increase* in journey time through design is not . . . well it would be sort of the antithesis of what we are trying to do. That sounds a little unhumanitarian. But that's pretty much what it's about.

Adesola: 'You've got to keep people moving' kind of thing?

> **Terry:** Yes, and even if you think about the spaces where we do design in places for people to spend time, it's generally with a view to them spending money as much as time.

Eric: I'm trying to think of the last time that I actually broke a journey when I was on business: I was going to a meeting near London Bridge. I had walked over from my station, walked over Tower Bridge and into that lovely area that is now between the GLA building and Tower Bridge where the theatre is, and I was early. I'm quite uncomfortable turning up places early because I'm not much of a conversationalist. So, I sat down in that nice little wooded area, but I went and bought myself a coffee to sit with, so there was that little commercial tag. There's a thing that I've seen on some YouTube channels recently, an advert, saying 'Make time to do nothing . . . [it's] a good use of your time'. I felt a bit like that. Not done it since though!

> **Adesola:** It's interesting that it is OK to stop if you've clearly got something you've purchased – like if you're standing with a coffee cup or you're standing eating or even staring in a shop window, picking something up to wonder if you're going to buy it, is approved wait time.

Terry: Whereas just to kind of stand there and 'be' would seem odd. This is partly what you made me think of when you were talking from an artistic point of view, there's sense in which waiting or preparation is part of creating art. I'm going to speak personally because I don't know how it is for other people, but for me more in the engineering world, it's very difficult to create a pause even in your own head. You're always conscious of what you're going to be doing next, so I know my next meeting is coming up at one, I've got another at three o'clock in [another part of the city] – in my day there isn't even a stillness in my mind.

> **Eric:** I think some of that is that, I'm sure you're very similar to me, that our work seems quite frenetic because

we're keeping lots of balls in the air at one time, and generally we're spending our time for the benefit of somebody else, so if you're a 'proper' professional you have a certain amount of pride in spending that time properly. Trying to put myself in an artistic, creative space, if I was there, I'd be doing it for me alone. So, spending that time just sitting there getting my brain in the right frame of mind, just trying to let the juices flow and almost switch off might be worthwhile time. But at work – you're constantly forward planning. Like I sat down in here and I started writing a to-do list, while I was waiting for you. While waiting. So even the dwelling has a forward momentum to it.

Terry: Exactly, after years and years that way of thinking seeps into who you are, and you can see how that perhaps seeps into the designs. There are some kinds of commercial and sort of cost/benefit reasons, but there's also the fact that that's how we think too, so that's probably how we expect other people to feel.

We discussed how it seems that the sensing body is used in two ways here. The logic of the city design is to keep people moving with 'dwell time' waits for needs that involve consumerism. Non-commercial waits do not seem logical. Reasonable activity during a pause in a journey, like to eat a sandwich from home, get water, toileting,[4] seem to be tolerable because they ultimately keep people moving. But any other sensory pause is regarded as a kind of luxury – art is positioned as something almost selfish – to be occupied by your own senses. To pause to smell something, look at the sky, touch the texture of a wall seems out of place. We discussed how public art attempts to be a sensory pause in the city, but at the cost of people feeling it is in their way or a waste of their time.

Later in the year, when dancers and I explored slowness and stillness on London Bridge as the sun rose, the majority of people walking across the bridge seemed quite affronted that we were there (also see Figure 4). Some people thought we were protesting, some felt they had licence to push us or swear at us. Only one person joined in with us, by raising rabbit ears behind me as a photo was taken! It was significant that art, feeling the sensory body, is perceived of as an almost selfish engagement with something. The drinking coffee, eating something, reading a book, window shopping nature of pauses give affluence the privilege of legitimate stopping.

It is easier to stop if you have money to spend. Within these pauses or stops, some people can stop more easily than others.

People do stop in Waterloo Station: at the top of the escalators!

Adesola: How do we control stillness in design?

> **Terry:** So, food and drink were the examples we used earlier.

Eric: I mean something that catches your eye. I mean, the stop – the pause – could be quite momentary, but it could still actually affect your journey that's maybe just one that you do all the while. An example: when I leave [work] I have to walk to [a major rail] station where that plaza area is. Sometimes they have advertising installations that sometimes are not even necessarily about advertising, they're some campaign that's happening – those tend to catch my attention. And I might walk that way around the space rather than the more direct one. Slow down a bit – not necessarily stop, because I'm on my way home.

> **Adesola:** So, people can stop – or slow down – if they are obviously doing something that is about the physicality of their body, like eating, drinking, looking, hearing. But if they're not obviously doing that then it starts to become *weird*.

Terry: Yes, yes.

> **Eric:** I'm not sure why you would stop if there wasn't some sensory benefit for it.

Adesola: But the question is: why would you *move* if there wasn't some sensory benefit also?

> **Eric:** I'm not sure if it necessarily works the other way around. To move there has to be something that's causing the impetus to make you move, that's cause and effect, isn't

it? You are only going to move if there is reason to move. But if you are already stopped, and there's no outside stimulus, you will just be on pause, and continue to be on pause.

Adesola: But the way everything is designed, it seems as if you don't start from *stop*, you start from *move*. It's almost like you need an impetus to stop.

> **Terry:** I agree. As soon as I get off the train at Waterloo, I wouldn't just stop in the middle of the concourse, if you see what I mean. I know that there's a flow, a direction I'm kind of supposed to take.

Eric: It's true, isn't it? Because you would only stop to check the time or check if I've got my wallet . . .

> **Terry:** . . . if I've still got my ticket.

Eric: The other thing is, you stop in the middle of Waterloo Station and you know that you're going to be in other people's way. I'd be conscious of that, also . . . Mind you, people do stop in Waterloo Station, at the top of the escalators!

> **Terry:** Or the bottom of escalators even!

Eric: But why do they do that? They do it because they're probably uncertain as to where they're going. . . . So that space, they're not reacting to that space properly. So, they're pausing through uncertainty.

> **Terry:** Or maybe they're reacting in a way that seems proper to them because they don't know, they're uncertain, but they're not reacting to it in the way that was anticipated when the space was designed.

Adesola: It's not a wandering stillness where you're responding to the place, it's a sort of fearful stillness isn't it?

A fearful stillness generated from a need to spatially re-evaluate where they are. Not to do with a sensory collaboration with environment. Talking with Eric, Larry and Terry raised questions about the qualities of stillness to explore (in the dance studio).

QUALITIES OF STILLNESS

In the dance studio:

> I step into the future of my right leg, muscles in my knee holding me in the present, as foot lifting reveals the past – grounded earth – and hip presses into the change that is about to transform the step into a balance. I am still, but only for the moment it takes before I lift my other leg behind me and I am still in the forever of that moment because that step is the atom in the arabesque. The minute adjustments that I continually make in order to dance the arabesque are each a momentary solution to the question of stillness. Heart pounds, the stillness of that moment is the balance: the question of stability and the catch of fall as I dance. I breathe into the arabesque, the assemblage of now, that has temporarily shaped into a balance. A breath out caresses the skin on the back of my hand. Extended fingers out before me: using the music as a lay line to stretch my fingertips along and toes conspire to join the stretch. I feel the warmth of bodies around me. I am within and without the fabric of my muscles as I begin to encounter the release of my heel to relevé. I am forever in this moment and this moment is gone within seconds. Floor music, muscle, dancers, breath; this place we have made *is*, and so I *am*. Dancing, I cannot perceive of stillness as interruption of movement – dancing stillness is perfect connection to all around, stillness that allows time to shift into space – a moment to be breath, floor, music, air on skin, walls and all this as one. Stillness when I dance is the connection to the between-ness of the past and future of now.

I talk with Sowmya Parthasarathy, urban designer (with a different international architectural firm than Eric, Larry and Terry). I ask her what stillness is.

Sowmya: Interesting question! I think you're right, a lot of what we do focuses on movement, vibrancy and activity and we prioritize things that allow people to meet and do things and come and go and you're right, we think less about standing still . . . one of the things that I think of when I think of stillness is that it's less to do with movement and more to do with acoustic quality. So, you can be very still and still walking somewhere, provided it's in a very quiet place, which I think we have less of in big cities. But we made a poster not very long ago about creating quiet spaces in cities and what that would mean. More and more children, who live in these multi-family neighbourhoods, don't have quiet places to study or sit in this crazy place. So, to me, when I close my eyes and think of a still place, I actually think of a quiet place, even if you're walking through it.

Adesola: A place to listen? I've noticed, there are some people, like homeless people for instance, where their stillness is antagonistic, in a sense.

Sowmya: Yes, I guess that's right. I suppose to me stillness is a little bit a state of mind, rather than movement. So, a homeless person can be sitting in the same place all day and really not be still because you're worrying where your meal is coming from, or what so-and-so is going to say, or about if you're going to be kicked out.

Adesola: That's what I mean by luxury, that not everyone has access to stillness. And I've noticed in a lot of the designs, there's a lot about accessing spaces, and moving to access spaces, but I'm wondering about how you access stillness.

Sowmya: In some ways it's not even a design question, it's more a question of philosophy where you can access stillness within yourself. I mean you can be quite still sitting on a bus stop bench. You don't really need the hidden Japanese garden around the corner, that would be nice, but if someone is so reliant on the ideal environment to find stillness then maybe it's not real stillness, because to me it's a state of mind. Yes, your environment can help you, and yes in those terms it's a luxury, because we all lead lives where we really have to steal those moments of stillness. But at least as designers we can facilitate, for those who have mental access to stillness, we can facilitate an environment where they can enjoy it.

Adesola: Do you think that art and things like dance are stillness?

Sowmya: I absolutely think so. I mean, I'm sure someone training for the Tour de France and riding a bike at fifty miles an hour can find stillness in that activity because it's almost meditative. And all of the creative activities, including dance, you might be moving but imagine when you're in the zone of it, you could find stillness, even if your body may be tired or you hear music or whatever.

Adesola: So, I think I'm hearing you say that in a way you're designing to facilitate people finding stillness in movement?

Sowmya: I think so, yes. I don't think a space does anything per say, it's a vessel, so you can design a park with beautiful trees and one person will be scared of trees and won't love it. . . . I would say designing those kinds of places, where people can have that moment with themselves, or with one other person, or with your cup of coffee or whatever . . . to me the really successful places are places that are rich in spaces where people, according to their little likes and dislikes, can have those punctuations in their daily routine. If you have none of that, then life is really boring and your environment isn't very rich.

Adesola: That's really beautiful. So, it's about the between-ness of experience?

Sowmya: Yes, and for different people it's different. So, for some people, it may be about going to a busy bar with friends or for someone it might be just sitting on that quiet bench in a park making a phone call.

A few months later I speak to Andrew Fraser, a journalist and author (Fraser, 2018), who has been homeless for over four years.

Andrew: Well, I'll speak as a homeless person, yeah, because I am still homeless. I was rough sleeping, I'm not rough sleeping now but I am still homeless – I don't have a home. I'm in temporary accommodation. In my time on the streets, which was on and off for three and a half years, I hardly ever experienced stillness because it was a constant battle with chaos – which is what it is, you're living in chaos. I guess people in the city are [living in chaos] as well in a different way, so the urge for stillness was huge. Ilford, where I'm going later, that was one of my first places on the streets. I slept behind the Marks & Spencer's store there, where they tortured us with the sound of a pigeon alarm all night because they wouldn't let us be still, we couldn't even sleep because we were vermin, so they would play this beep, beep, beep all night; it would drive you insane. My friend, who has just come off the streets yesterday, is massively sleep deprived. I mean, hopefully he'll sleep all weekend, I did – I slept for, like, three days when they put me into a room. What I used to do was – I was lucky in Ilford, because there's a place called Valentine's Park, which is beautiful, and ancient – I was homeless there in the sort of summertime and springtime, so I would go there, and it just totally changed my energy, really –

Adesola: Is that around the stillness of the place?

Andrew: Yes. Yes, yes. I'd go and find my favourite tree there and I'd go and sit by the tree and the wishing well, and I'd be at one with nature. I'd take my shoes off and my socks off and feel my feet on the grass, which is really important because you're kind of earthing yourself, you know, and if I spent a couple of hours in there, I would be energetically rejuvenated and I would be able to go and face more chaos. So, yeah, certainly for homeless people, stillness is kind of essential, but also you get addicted to the adrenaline and to the chaos and I think that perhaps, like I say, if you're in the city, that's kind of similar, you know? Everyone's running around, yapping orders at each other, whatever . . .

Adesola: I have been thinking that stillness isn't lack of movement, it's something to do with connection.

Andrew: Yeah. It is, but you have to be in the right environment. I mean some people can drop into the *zone* of method meditation and things like that and do it anywhere but we're standing here in Barking, London, right now and let me tell you, it's not called Barking for nothing, you know? It really is *barking*, it's extremely hard to find stillness 'round here.

As we talk, Andrew is repeating what Sowmya says about stillness being to do with state of 'mindful body'. I feel we are all in agreement of seeing 'stillness' as being about active engagement in sensory connection to what is around, to *Place*. Transaction: shaping and welcoming being shaped by environment. It seems stillness – to be spatially present – is treated as a privilege in the city. Andrew talks about daydreams of an art installation where homeless people could go and be safe to just feel.

After these conversations I think to myself, homeless people are far from still – they are vibrating so fast they almost *appear* still to those of us not homeless. The privilege the city offers some people is to be still – be a part of it all – but this is only offered to those for whom the design of the buildings reaches out to readily. If you are in sync for a moment with the purpose of the building or the flow of the movement around it, you might be able to take a moment to be a part of it all. If what you are doing does not meet the purpose of the design, then you cannot be still.

Andrew: . . . I used to hand out cakes to people. I used to go and buy millionaire's shortbread – which was my little joke with myself – and I'd sit there and I'd say 'oh it's role reversal day today, would you like a cake?' 'Would you like a cake?' And they'd be like, 'what do you want?' and 'I'd say nothing, just take a cake, go on please, enjoy it'. And I didn't care if they didn't give me anything for it, that wasn't the purpose, but some people would be kind enough to throw you a 50p or a quid or something and some people would just sit down and chat. This lovely Asian girl used to come down and we used to chat every night and she'd tell me about her life and ask me if should she date this guy or that guy . . . and there was a lovely older couple who used to come down the steps every night with lots of bags – I think they must have had their own restaurant but they obviously weren't wealthy otherwise they would have been in a taxi – and they had huge bags of vegetables every day so I used to run to the top of the stairs and carry it down for them. Really, when I stopped doing that I really worried if someone else would step in and do it for them but yeah, it became a spiritual space.

Adesola: Do you think that art creates those kinds of spaces?

Andrew: Yes, definitely. I mean art is a civilizing thing, you know? I think art is the answer to so many questions. It really is.

Adesola: But why?

Andrew: Because it takes people out of themselves and it lets them focus on something else and it could have different meanings for different people. And again, it gives them that pause for contemplation which is such a rare commodity these days.

Stillness starts to fit with the framework of *Place* through being an awareness of the present moment. What Dewey calls the *situation*: to be a part of it all. I notice that design could be challenged to ask if the buildings of the city are designed to reach out to some people while others are left with incidental connections, or even asked to change themselves in order to connect. It is also a criticism for dance to look at how the works we create connect with some people all the time but expect others to change themselves to connect with our work (even if this just means we dancers expect them to come to a theatre space to find us). For me, choreographically, these lessons in stillness are about taking the interconnected knowledges I feel when I dance – the *Place*-making my choreography attempts – and asking how I see them in world around when they are not looked for. I can recognize a connection with the world when I am dancing but how is this connection manifested in the city – how does the city dance? It seems the performance of the city, performing architecture, involves how we conceive of and offer stillness – connection. How we are beyond ourselves in the *Places* we inhabit, noticing the marks we and others leave and being attentive to the ways the buildings shape us, witnessing how we are opened up.

BEING A PART OF THE STREET THROUGH STILLNESS WITH IT

I explore choreographing a dance that juxtaposes three speeds of the city: the speed of traffic, the slow presence of the buildings, and myself dancing. I use the *Isadora*[5] computer programme to film, which allows me to play with how stillness and movement are captured. I am dancing in a street at the side of the British Library near traffic lights. The traffic lights facilitate capturing traffic passing me at stops and starts. I move very slowly from one aesthetic shape to another. Behind me is a city building whose lines my shapes are reflecting. I film my dance using the *Isadora* programme, coded so that the camera only captures very slow movement and stillness: movement is captured as blur. As I dance the film captures how I dance in and out of rhythm with that around me. As people and traffic slow to my speed they appear clearly in the dance film. When things move quickly, they blur. DancingStrong Movement Lab artists Harry and intern Lauren McGonagle film me.

FIGURE 7 A. Akinleye dancing in the street documentation. Photo H. Fulleylove (also see *On Dwelling* film included in Figure 12's QR code link).

Spatial acts of presence, stillness as presence

Earlier, I discussed the emplaced/embodied *Being-in-Place* framework I am working from. Using Dewey's lexicon, this is a framework of a world in a transactional relationship. A rejection of dualist separations such as mind/body and subject/object is 'mindfulness' replaced by a 'mind-ful-body-in-environment'. Within this framework, explorations of stillness seem to present themselves as moments of awareness of being a part of it all, *Mitakuye Oyasin*, being in *Place*. Stillness from my choreographic perspective is about connection, nowness – Dewey expresses this as 'experience': being present for 100 per cent of the moment. It is less about 'movement in time' and more about 'relationship'. Stillness becomes about finding a relationship with world around. It is not about the apparent change in rhythm of movement slowing or stopping produces. Here, stillness is less in terms of rhythm and more in terms of relationships – to be relationally with that which is around us. This is a shift from thinking temporally to thinking spatially. I also note what Scott L. Pratt has suggested in his email correspondence (also cited in Part One).

> Rather than organizing one's self-understanding and relations with others temporally (and in the context of a kind of universal time), I proposed that American Indian traditions suggest that meaning can be organized spatially. This, of course, does not rule out sequences of events, but rather holds that their meaning is a matter of the 'spatial' relations that are instantiated in the sequences.
>
> *(from personal email correspondence with* **S. PRATT,** *May 2011)*

As I think spatially, not temporally, as Pratt suggests and the conversations expose, my choreographic explorations foreground relationships. The relationship is primary.

I and some artists from DancingStrong Movement Lab go to London Bridge in the early morning as a place where there are patterns of movement (people travelling to work in the city) have been designed as part of the urban development of the area (follow Figure 4's QR code link). I am interested in the patterns of relationships the pedestrians make as they criss-cross the bridge as areas swell with people in some moments and spaces re-emerge at others. I am thinking about the relationship of my body to the buildings in the distance, the lines and shapes we make together and the relationship I have with the other dancers and people crossing the bridge. I am conceiving of myself in terms of my relationship with what is around me. For me, the choreographic interest is in the relationships between people and things that makes the dancing appear. From an urban designer's point of view, it seems they would look at how flow cannot be interrupted, how pathways can be managed to keep the people moving without any disruption of the dominate rhythm, pace. They would engage with London Bridge by thinking temporally rather than spatially. It seems that, for them, rhythm is at the forefront as a single possibility for what to do with the bridge – march across it in a single relationship with it – conceiving of oneself in terms of how you keep up with the flow of moving people. Any other relationship with the bridge, other than the rhythmic march of people across it, is hard to connect with. In thinking about *Chasing Stillness*, I am noticing the same entry point of time/rhythm being used again and again and seeing how design becomes habitual. The spatial approach of relationships here is lost.

Weaving ideas – possessing the ground

I have asked, is home the only place you can be still? Is 'stillness' the only way to be home?

We are in transaction with environment around.
Our perception of environment shapes it and us.

The *Logic of Place* is conceived by Pratt in order to denote the point that the environment indicates how it is engaged with.

Together the matrix of mindful body–environment offers logic to moving around. Of course, this largely focuses on the implications of understanding oneself and others in spatial terms. Part of the matrix of the building of the city involves the designers who shape the structure of the city.

The art of the design is part of the shaping of *Place* and part of the *Logic of Place*. To be present in *Place* to have the possibility of *Chasing Stillness* is easier when the design of the building or city is aimed at a rhythm that creates a relationship that fits your identity. When it is not, one can become invisible in the rush of the patterns of logic that people and buildings are using to create each other. For those not in the predominate rhythm, finding meaningful relationship with *Place* takes much concentration (as rhythm and relationship are in continuum).

Art's work is to be out of place and yet by being out of place it challenges what possibilities *Place* can be.

Filmmaker Anton Califano and I go to London Bridge so he can film me dancing with the rhythm of sunrise. Dancing on London Bridge, it was as if my rejection of the predominate relationship (walk-to-work) was being pounded into me. Stepping out of that rhythm gives permission for objectifying, for *any* relationship, to be imposed onto me. Design produces space but it also produces meaning for that space. When my dancing body is slowly moving in time with the light of the rising sun on London Bridge, my relationship with the bridge seems incomprehensible to those around me. People passing by feel legitimate in knocking into me, speaking to me, getting angry – some people assume I am protesting. I have stepped out of the expected organization of the rhythm of the bridge. By being in this distinctly different sunrise rhythm, I have placed myself as *available* to be interacted with because I am exhibiting a redefinable set of rules of behaviour (Goffman, 1980). I am open to reinterpretation, objectification. This sunrise dance on London Bridge is an artwork because I have chosen to interrupt the rhythm and have displaced it to find a different relationship with bridge. In a sense, it *is* a protest but in that sense all art could be seen as a protest. It is as if my not-fitting-in needs to be externally organized for me. My Black, female body becomes open by its 'otherness' (open, undeveloped, exposed, public, gaping, amendable, unlocked).

Developing this further, Harry Fulleylove, Maga Radlowska-Judd and I take some rehearsals into the streets to *chase* the stillness (connection) of different places in London (Charing Cross, Soho and Hendon). In dancing, we are outside of the designed rhythm; people feel that we are out of *Place*, allowing them to comment on our presence, to objectify us. We become present on their terms, not our own. When we are just walking to get somewhere else to dance, people are silent and polite, but out of step, by dancing, attempting to find our embodied stillness (connection) with places, somehow gives them permission to objectify with us – we become part-owned, open and trivialized.

Those bodies outside the connectedness of the designed rhythm are more liable to unwelcome emotional and physical interaction – the psychic danger of losing a sense of relationship with oneself that Andrew describes in being homeless. Bodies out of the dominant rhythm are liable to relationships that are more exposed and, at the same time, selfhood becomes less visible. In this way the rhythm of cities is classed/gendered/racialized because they design for some rhythms and those out of that rhythm are vulnerable to any relationship imposed on them. Where the interest lies in the *Choreographing the City: as/at the city limits* project is

FIGURE 8 H. Fulleylove and M. Radlowska-Judd dancing on the street R&D, July 2019. Photo: A. Akinleye.

that some identities interrupt the designed rhythm and are therefore out of (the correct) relationship with the design, purely by way of who they are perceived to be. It is not a choice to step out of the dominant rhythm/relationship: the perceived relationship is not one that they can be a part of. As a result, what was my *art*, my *protest*, becomes unconsciously embodied in my identity – my Black female body, Andrew's queer 'homeless' body, this person's wheelchair-using body, that person's ageing body, the identities of such people become romanticized, erotized or villainized purely because they are seemingly open to objectification as they are not a part of the urban geographic rhythm planned for a space.

In *Demonic Grounds: Black Women And The Cartographies Of Struggle*, human geographer Katherine McKittrick suggests Black women are treated as if they were 'un-geographic' (McKittrick, 2006, p. xiii). I think of Andrew's queering of the morning flow at the tube station with his cakes, interrupting the rhythm by redefining the relationship he has with the people passing by; how he says it was so hard for people to readjust to a different relationship with him through comments of 'I don't have any money, mate' and his answer 'I don't want any'. Andrew's Queering of the relationship with passer-by challenged the un-geographic of his homeless body in the design of the train station. This highlights how spatial relationship with built environment renders some identities geography-less (such as non-white, Queer, working-class, female and / or non-mainstream bodies). For instance, the geography of the possible relationships of walk-to-work on London Bridge becomes the habitat that co-creates the narrative of work. A habitat established by the relationships one can have with the design that nurtures some bodies and rhythms of Self while suppressing others. The co-created relationship between Self and built environment is verified by the only rhythm designed for – the rhythm of walk-to-work. The only person you can be is walk-to-work-person, and work carries with it the exclusion the design of the bridge. The rhythm of walk-to-work is not neutral, it is storied – peppered with expectation of your relationship with others as you join the rhythm.

I am remembering that a relationship (for instance bridge-to-walk-work/ worker) is not the momentary *nowness* I have suggested is found with the connection of 'stillness'. The singular rhythm involves a constructed history and future. In the designed/facilitated rhythm of the morning track to work across London Bridge, we assume bridge was and will be for professionals to get to the city – 'worker' who is settled in 'job', is dependable, is not about to be made redundant. The relationship the facilitated rhythm offers involves a whole reality and general relationship. The opposite of the ever-changing, responsive, connection of 'stillness'.

I consider that for those who are not in the predominate rhythm, finding *relationship* is a process of having to possess the ground – claim space.

> racism and sexism produce attendant geographies that are bound up in human disempowerment and dispossession. . . . Bodily violence spatializes other locations of dehumanization and restraint, rendering bodily self-possession and other forms of spatial ownership virtually unavailable to the violated subject.
>
> (**MCKITTRICK,** 2006, p. 3)

McKittrick has argued that Black women's experiences are perceived of as *un-geographic* because they are peripheral or invisible to the predominate meaning-making of the mapping of histories. Their experience is not given a geography because it has been made incidental by the narrative meaning-making of colonial, misogynic understanding of the relationships that have brought us to the period of *now*. Following this, I am suggesting the design of many spaces has become un-rhythmic for some people's bodies: un-rhythmic and therefore relationship-less, other than a relationship which involves taking on a projected identity.

The luxury of *Chasing Stillness* is the ability to *feel* myself into *Place*. Stillness to reach out and find how we (elements of *Place* including 'I') fit together. The challenge to design is to create the tentacles of possibility that offer multiple ways in, and to create the spaces to proposition stillness to do this.

A dance to be made: the poetics of body on *Demonic Grounds*

My choreographic notes for making a piece about *Chasing Stillness*:

Walking quickly to catch the train or following the flow of people to the coffee shop area I quieten to become present, to arrive in *Place*. I move at the pace it takes for me to become present. The choreographer moves at the pace it takes to be present in each step, to feel the somatic extension of skin to brick, brick to skin – the edges of the dancer transform to join the aesthetic of the built surroundings. *Chasing Stillness*(es) seems to offer explorations for being present – to be aware of multiple spatial locators – to know you are in more than one relationship at once – to be more fully contextualized than the one relationship dictated by the dominant rhythm (that is most often white-straight-male-middle-class) offers.

Choreographically, I become interested in how to create work that brings dancers, audience and environment into multiple unexpected aesthetic relationships with each other. To reveal the many spatial relationships one has at any moment as a part of locating who we are.

I consider how a geography, a map or a blueprint of the city buildings is not a documentation of something that just *is*, they are attempts to tame the complexities of human experiences – the joys, truths, griefs, fears, hopes of contextualizing the sensation of meaning-making.

Sensation responds to environments and so we produce spaces, meanings and identities in partnership, in transaction with the ground we stand on. And thus, cities and buildings are alive. McKittrick suggests the grounds become demonic because of the unknowable of 'otherness', or become demonic because of my unfolding. *Demonic* refers to the capability of spirits, demons, deities to possess a human being. The demonic is the attribute of the human or object through which the spirit is making itself present (rather than the demon itself). This demonic is in the transaction, the procession.

I am seeing each building as possessing a spirit (demonically present or felt when we interact with them) created by the relationships that are created/permitted with it. McKittrick's use is intended to shift the response to demonic from fearful unknowable to the development of an awareness of the unfolding of the possession as a vantage point outside the map. What the design is, what we are, is not revealed in the blueprint but emerges through the way the *it* is used. 'It' is because 'we' are revealed through how the design possesses and is possessed by people. When I become unknowable Black woman in the corridor, the corridor becomes possessed by the injustice of my invisibility. I become possessed by the 'otherness' of being invisible/unknowable.

Possessing the street after ballet class

After taking a ballet class in London I often take the longer route of going south to Piccadilly Circus to get the train because I love the lights and traffic and potential of the centre of London. Today, I walk past the train station and continue down Regent Street, turn right on Jermyn Street, pass shops and a church and then turn left again on to Duke of York Street. I am looking for the house Sarah Baartman (Saartjie Baartman) lived in at the beginning of the 1800s (Holmes, 2008). Sarah Baartman was an artist from South Africa, born around 1789. She was brought to England where she performed on stage to an audience that was obsessed with her 'difference'. European crowds fetishized her female Black body, particularly her buttocks and thighs. The managers she was contracted to work for targeted audiences to attend shows more in the vein of freak show attraction than seeing Sarah as an artist. But Sarah's resistance was her singing and dancing which illustrated her persistence in trying to create on her own terms. Sarah was presented in public shows and also hired out for private shows where while she sang her songs; she was measured, touched and examined by the social classes (Holmes, 2008). Dehumanized, passed around, persecuted and placed on display to perform for up to twelve hours a day, Sarah's short life blueprinted a continued aggression through the objectification of Black female bodies.

Using McKittrick's Black feminist approach, city geography is underscored by the social production of space. The physicality of this social production of space holds my limbs tightly now, restricts my breath as I stare at the town house buildings Sarah would have lived in. I consider how, even after her death in 1815, Sarah's body parts were put on display in Paris. In 1994, negotiations for her remains to be returned to South Africa to be given a burial were begun by President Nelson Mandela. Some 187 years after her death, she was buried in 2002. I wonder at how she would have felt the cold London wind that blows under my woollen hat as I walk back up the street where Sarah's house was to the theatre in Piccadilly where she performed. In a copy of an illustration of the original advertisement for Sarah's show the address given for the theatre is 225 Piccadilly (Holmes, 2008). As I walk past the Hard Rock Café in Piccadilly looking for the building numbers, a man who is stopping people to raise funds against knife crime says to me: 'Namaste, is that how you say it?' I say, 'I think so', and keep on walking. He calls after me – 'where are you from?' I say, 'Here, London'. I realize I am pointing my finger at the ground. 'No, where are you originally from?' I think of my red-haired grandma and her grandma all living in North London: I am too far away to answer him now as I disappear into the crowd. As I find the numbers of the building hidden behind shopping signs, it looks as if what is now the Hard Rock Café was where the theatre must have been. So, I end up walking back past the man again. He has noticed my stillness saying, 'you don't look like you are from here'. My stopping to feel this place, feeling for Sarah here, makes me seem like I do not belong. Tourists have permission to stop and feel the place, I suppose. I say, 'I am', and take me and my notions of Sarah down Shaftesbury Avenue to one of my favourite bubble tea shops for a hot drink before I take the tube home.

The walk from ballet class to Duke of York Street is my own unique map of London. The history of my persistence in taking ballet classes despite rejection of my Black body's capability to dance is etched in the paving stones I have walked on over the years. Old comments that my teenage butt and thighs and my hair would be too big for ballet, despite my small frame, carve the way I held my body and the way I have walked to class for the past thirty years. Roads and alleyways that shared the story of my growth and frustrations as I step onto them, heavy hearted or light from returning to London after dancing in the USA. The geography of Sarah's Piccadilly shaped me unknowingly, a significance invisible to the predominant natives of the City of London. McKittrick points to how my bodily expression here has been possessed by 'Sarah on display'. The streets to ballet are demonic.

When I arrive on a city street as a Black female body, I arrive into a history/present/future. I arrive into the lived identity of the dominant relationship predetermined by the design of the street – a design that is rarely created to support a relationship with the lived experience of the identity I that have.

I dream of responsive architecture that is demonic because it is alive, porous, reaching out, aware of its ability to possess a human being (McKittrick, 2006, p. xxiv). Aware of where its determinations, concealments, marginalizations and boundaries lie and understanding that these places, although un-geographic, are not un-designed. The shift is that the demonic design is the willingness to be schizophrenic and witness itself producing multiple meanings and relationships with the people it collaborates with to make *Place*.

Beginning by housing *moments* of 'stillness' where relationships can be forged, negotiated, felt.

Lessons in stillness suggest to me that there are people whose experiences are made un-geographic because their experiences are outside the predominate rhythm of the flow of the city design. They are unknowable because the relationship they have with the city is spatially hidden by the rhythm of the movement around them. Their experience blurs into the buildings and they are only noticed when the vibration or frequency of their movements interrupts the flow to disturb, for a moment, the rhythm of the design – some people stop at the top of the escalators at Waterloo Station!

As I listen, in verbal and movement conversations, I want to remain attentive to the way what we are saying (and what I am making) fits with the *Being-in-Place* framework. By its nature, this embodied perspective rejects dualist divides and binaries such as mind and body, subject and object, time and space. Instead, these binaries are replaced with spectrums and continuums. Rhizomic models replace linear structures for organizing ideas. Mind and body are shifted to Dewey's 'mindful body', subject and object dissolve into transactional knower–known (Dewey and Boydston, 1989).

Place involves time and space, as for the embodied being time and space are not separated. Tongan notions of *Tā* (loosely translated as 'rhythm') and *Vā* (loosely translated as 'relationship') offer language that moves me away from the dualist limits of time and space (Akinleye and Kindred, 2018; Māhina, 2004). Starting to conceive of the embodied notion of no separation between time and space, I take steps into the Tongan concept of *Tā/Vā* ('rhythm'/'relationship') (Māhina, 2002, 2004; Wendt, 1999). As rhythm and relationships are revealed through conversations and through the city, it is through using *Tā/Vā* as a methodology for examining ideas that I attempt to remain grounded in movement. But *Tā/Vā* comes from a Tonga Indigenous world view that becomes oversimplified if we attempt to separate *Tā* and *Vā* from each other. I am not suggesting that rhythm (*Tā*) and relationship (*Vā*) are separate elements, rather they are interconnected, more like Dewey's 'entry points' into understanding or being aware of the *now*.

The 'otherness' of racial, socio-economic, gendered matters are spatial matters – movements. Regulations that uphold the hierarchical structures that validate them predominantly regulate bodies in terms of the times and spaces they can occupy – rhythms of the dance of the city. I have proposed that from an embodied perspective (space) spatial matters are relational – towards relationship (*Vā*) in the rhythm–relationship harmony. Relationship/relational/spatial is the historical/present/future expectations of what we are creating each other as.

As I participate in and reflect on the conversations, I am using the idea of *rhythm* to indicate personality – identity, the unique cadence of a *thing* that makes it distinguishable. I am using the idea of *relationship* as identity in terms of how you are constructed by what is around you.

Chasing Stillness seems to be about a disharmony between rhythm and relationship where one dominant rhythm is over-privileged, making it hard to have another kind of relationship with the city than the one the dominant rhythm dictates.

Thus, one steps out of the spatial prescription – *steps out of pace* – to *chase stillness* in order to find or feel other possible relationships.

Design and choreography are tasked with making it easier to have these moments of stillness – connection to now, to find how you are connected, how you can be connected – of *Place*, to acknowledge the multiple possibilities of identities (rhythms) of the city. To be in partnership with the spatial, in order to notice and acknowledge the multiple relationships you are in; to notice the grace of the historied, potential relationships you want or that are indicated by your *Being* in this *Place*.

Desire Lines 1

My body is an archive of everything I've touched, every relationship made. The walls of this city are in my blood as I melt into them. Take my place as unknowable 'Black woman in the crowd'.

My body is the archive of 'Sarah on display', of the astonishing, stranger that crowds the streets. I dissolve into the heat of the city complexly sweet and invisible as Tate and Lyle's sugar.

My body is documented by a thousand cameras a day. City vigilance that controls my non-presence; that makes sure I appear only where I can be captured.

My body fragments into a million gigabytes and my femininity is made real by the stare of the security guard, visibility in the light of the pixel. I am coded into acknowledgment: data that says my Blackness was there.

Excited by ideas of *Chasing Stillness* and the conversations I have had with people and *Places*, I enter the dance studio and start to choreograph . . .

5 LINGERING IN DWELLING, RESIDING IN WANDERING

Previously, *Chasing Stillness* was about the spatial ability to co-create relationship with [. . .] through stepping beyond the dominant/prescribed rhythm to find a Self authentically renewing with *Place*. This was to notice an imbalance of rhythm and relationship where a single rhythm dominates spatial possibilities, whereas *Lingering in Dwelling, Residing in Wandering* became about an imbalance of rhythm and relationship where one single relationship is over-privileged. The problem it highlights is a temporal one, a stagnation that only accommodates my presence as a singular occasion, a singular relational vibration/resonance to my presence. The theme of *Lingering in Dwelling, Residing in Wandering* suggests development of design and/or choreography that nurtures/responds to an ability to co-create across the expanse of time, not to limit our relationship with city to something galvanized at one particular moment and left in that moment.

Standing in a tunnel in Whitechapel, I tap out a rhythm on my body and hear it bounce back to me from the tunnel wall in front of me. Timing that tells me I am standing near the tunnel wall. Each time I move I listen for the one echo that tells me I am standing near the wall. I become (the relationship of wall–woman). I only know myself from the rhythm it takes for my presence to be bounced back by wall. *Lingering in Dwelling, Residing in Wandering* I tap my movement and my rhythm comes back to me at different times at once: a polyrhythmic echo describing me (who has been only wall–woman until that time) in terms of possibilities of the whole landscape, not just wall, the multiple relationships that place me. *Dwelling/Wandering* become about to be with [. . .] through the accessibility of the polyrhythms of Place of which my body contributes and becomes.

Dwelling/Wandering are constructed here as finding the polyrhythms of *Place* to understand the multiple relationships I am a part of. *Dwelling* resides in the sense that one can wander the cord, the harmony of time, to discover the cadence of *Being-in-Place*.

I go beyond mySelf, 'I' am 'we', 'we' are environment, ancestors, dreams – time is not a line we meander along. Time is the polyrhythms of our relationships.

A conversation about wandering

Civil engineer Eric looks at his phone and says his next meeting has been delayed so he can stay to talk a little longer. I am so grateful to Eric and his colleague, technical director Terry, for their support for the *Choreographing the City* project through giving me time to improvise ideas with them.[1] Our conversations play with ideas verbally in the same way the dancers Harry, Maga, Lauren and musician Jake have been exploring movement ideas with me in the dance studio. Having spoken about stillness I ask Eric and Terry about the 'stillness of home'. This leads our conversation into a drift, where we wander ideas about vacation and time.

Meeting Eric and Terry again after thinking about *Lingering in Stillness* I ask them: 'Is home the only place you can be still?'

Eric: My wife and I have started having quite a lot of long weekends away, rather than having big block holidays [vacations]. We've been hanging around – we like to go and see live music. Why go and see that music in London? Why don't we go and see that band in Cambridge or in Bristol and stay over for that weekend? And that getting away from my usual environment, which is 'round here, that takes all that busy fuzziness out of my head as well. It's sort of like taking the lid off your head a little bit.

Terry: I think that would be true for me too. Because my first instinct when you said, 'Is home the only place you can be still?' was 'Yes, it probably is'. But I was thinking about that in contrast to coming to London to do work, but there's loads of places where we're still; if we go away on holiday [vacation], or if we go to a city for some reason other than for work. Because you could sit in a café and just watch people go by for an hour or something and it would be great. So, I think for me, I can be still in other places but it's a question of what mode I'm in: whether it's more work or away from work.

Adesola: Do you think that's something to do with being in other places, that you're not as familiar with what sort of movement you're meant to be doing? So, you're more able to kind of resist it?

> **Eric:** Perhaps the movement that you end up making has not been pre-thought out. It's just you react to the place.

Terry: Yeah.

> **Eric:** We were in Cambridge a couple of weekends ago and we arrived at our hotel early. The room was ready, so we checked in and had the whole day [ahead], pretty much, everything from about eleven o'clock for the rest of the day, to ourselves. And we literally just bumbled around the place and 'Oh, look at that!', 'Look at that!'

Terry: It's a different kind of movement, isn't it? 'Shall we go down this street?', 'have a look down there?' You never do that in a city normally if you come for work, I never would.

> **Eric:** And just letting inspiration carry you somewhere, almost like Brownian motion – you're just being knocked about by how you interact to what's around you. Probably on a subconscious level. A little bit of architecture captures your eye and you go to focus on that, or 'What's that group of people doing over there?', 'What's that brightly coloured thing?'

Terry: Maybe there's a market or something?

> **Eric:** Yeah, the market. We ended up at the market, which is probably natural city design, it focuses you in. But I think it is a different sort of city design because it's not pre-planned. In coming here today, I've followed one of two or three routes I can use to come here. Large parts of those routes being pre-determined by railway lines and what have you.

Adesola: So, when you design things do you design one or two routes, or do you try and design lots of alternatives to get to places?

> **Eric:** Sometimes you have to design lots of different routes as options for other people to give an opinion on.

Adesola: I mean the final thing though; is the final design optimum when it's got a lot of things, or is it more optimum when there's a clear single ...

> **Terry:** It's usually the one, isn't it?

Eric: It's all about reducing scope.

> **Terry:** So, you might start with a lot of choices but you're looking to narrow it down to one and say, 'This is the thing we're going to do and this is how people will get from here to there'.

Adesola: ... because one of the things that I came to think about after we' did some dancing about urban dwelling was sort of what you're saying: that dwelling can be wandering. ... What about the rules of a place, like the logic of a space? What are your thoughts on – within your practises – of the idea of the logic of space or the rules of a place?

> **Eric:** Rules are what engineering is all about. It is using man-made rules to shape the human environment ... the natural environment, rather. So, we are governed by them. And they're rules of physics and they're rules of economy. We keep coming back to this association of what we do with money.

Terry: Yes, it's hard to disconnect that, isn't it?

> **Eric:** Completely. Yes, it doesn't necessarily sit well, given that we're meant to be improving society, quality of life, we're actually, ultimately improving the public purse, I suppose. But if I'm designing something that would happen, such as out of my team, we've just put in now our proposal for [a road improvement], it's about improving road safety, safety for pedestrians, improving journey times for buses and cyclists at the detriment of cars. It's focusing on more modern, sustainable modes over the more traditional, old fashioned ones. So, you will have a want to try and reduce the number of options that are open to people, so that their movement is pre-ordained to what you would say would be the fastest and the safest places to

be at any one time. You want people to cross the road at a safe place rather than just at free will. You want cyclists to be at a certain part of the width of the road rather than just anywhere. So, yes, I think we do create our own rules to define the logic that then happens.

Terry: Yes, and that happens in relation to what's already there [legally], because we're not starting from nothing.

Eric: Yes, we have lots of constraints.

Terry: There's a lot of constraints as well, you know. And I think there's also something about, if you start to design urban spaces and you didn't have those rules, the questions about what is an appropriate design would be a lot harder to interpret, they'd be much broader. There's something about having rules that focus and channel the possibility, isn't there? If someone says 'Oh, I object to this proposal. I would prefer you to do it this way' one of the responses is 'We can't do it that way because that's against the codes we have to comply with'. So, there's something – I don't quite know what the word is – directive? Protective? There's something that steers the choices that are made through the existence of those rules.

Eric: Your palette of materials, if you like . . .

Terry: . . . is constrained. That's right, you can't just do whatever you want.

Eric: . . . is pre-determined from that start. Yes, you can't use green paint; the rules say you only use red, blue and yellow.

Adesola: So, a good design is when you can make the rules feel like a natural logic. Is that right?

Eric: Well, that would be a fantastic result.

Terry: It would be, yes. If you could that would be quite a good design.

Eric: Because even though there are rules there, they're never going to suit everybody. They're just designed to suit an average situation. You don't design a road to cater for a lunatic that drives at 250 miles per hour. But you do design a road for a certain amount of –

Terry: Yes, so you make an allowance.

> **Eric:** – driving over the speed limit. Likewise, you don't design it for people who crawl along at twenty miles per hour on a motorway.

Terry: There are these bands that we're sort of expected to exist and fit within.

> **Eric:** I think where these rules blur, though, is where you are designing what you might call a 'traditional space'. So, I mentioned the market in Cambridge, or now, say, a pedestrianized high street. They're more permeable and they're more – I've mentioned Brownian motion – people just being knocked about by other molecules, if you like. That happens more. I'm not that sort of designer, so this is my opinion rather than fact, but I think that now people will try and design those spaces such that you don't take the most direct route through them –

Terry: Yes.

> **Eric:** – and that you will wander. And it might be a reduction in your speed of travel as you get to that area, even if you're just travelling through it. I hope that's the case.

Later, I consider how we went from *home* to *vacation* in the conversation. I wander if this is because we feel more at home in ourselves when we are on vacation as a result of having a more open canvas for who we can be. The places we visit offer different relationships to us because we are building them for the first time (or re-building them after time away). Time seems to move differently on vacation than during the working week.

Permeable, hovering

I am in the dance studio with Helen Kindred who is researching for her PhD work . . . *Whispers*. We are exploring the idea of connection between each other and dance studio space. We have been improvising using the idea of hovering (see Figure 4's QR code link). I have been thinking of hovering in terms of a hovercraft which pushes air down against a surface to create a current of air it moves along, as if hovering is to use the tension/ energy at the very edge of interaction (for instance between river and metal of hovercraft) to be in/on the air. We wonder about using the lenses of elements to explore hovering as a movement exercise – we are familiar with an 'air' type hovering. I consider water-hovering and think of those insects that move using the tension of the water surface. I wonder, what would earth-hovering be? To be in/on the soil. I lay on the studio floor and consider dissolving into the linoleum – like an insect that moves across the surface of sand by moving the tiny granules around and behind it. I try to find a softness to my body attempting to move by pouring my weight from limb through floor to limb, a permeable body, a permeable floor. I think about Pina Bausch's *Rite of Spring* and the way the earth floor it is performed on becomes a part of the dance as dancers move in and on it and it clings to their sweaty skin as the pace and urgency of the dance progresses.

I explore movement I call earth-hovering on the floor and walls of the studio. I come to this influenced by the city-wandering conversations I have been having. For me, choreographically earth-hovering/city-hovering seems to be about compliance, and acquiescence without disappearance.

I clasp into the hard wall, use it to soften my skin into permeability with its form and at the same time reshape the edges of the room through the presence of my body. Moving with wall becomes a negotiation of my weight in terms of the limitations, the shape of smooth straight wall folding ninety degrees into floor and redirecting at corner. In the fast rhythm of the rehearsal studio it seems only dancer is reshaped but in the slower rhythm of the year of rehearsal in this space dancers' repeated use of areas of the room are reshaping the room (what would be called the 'wear and tear' of the room). Over time my presence, the rhythm of my movements, of stopping, pausing and going, that instigates my dancing, shapes the room also.

How I use the room is in adherence to the relationship I can have with it (free for two hours every Thursday morning). The edits of interaction across time shape the room as my use of it becomes a rhythmic weekly engagement. Where there is repeated use, floor ground is reshaped. Rhythms of movement possibility I had not noticed the room could offer become lost by the habit of my interaction with it. In a two hour rehearsal rhythm, the body is more materially reshaped (sometimes I leave rehearsal bruised, as I have hit the floor inexpertly). In a year-long use rhythm, the room is more materially reshaped. I see this reshape and conforming of my dancing body and room as a negotiation through time, as the dialogue reflecting a dance has with environment more generally. In dialogue, dancer and environment are in a relationship of incompleteness, constantly changing each other at each encounter.

Dwelling and wandering as acts of willing incompleteness

In the West, generally, incompleteness often reads as uncomfortable. But it seems that to dwell and wander on vacation is to be in an incomplete relationship with the journey you are on – one that is permeable, that can be added to by something catching your eye, or an interesting smell or colour, 'what are those people doing?' Eric and Terry talked about wandering on vacation as breaking away from being in a complete, closed, designed cycle (such as travel to work and back).

When creating a site-specific dance, I begin choreographically by looking at where I can be in dialogue with the elements of the building. Where can the dance be present that allows the building to have an incompleteness, that the moment of the artist being there adds to, connects to? I am looking for points of incompleteness I can be in dialogue with through the dance artwork. The act of *hovering* being in/on the building is heightened by the senses, as site-specific dance highlights the blur of edges between building and artists – the artwork dwells with the [. . .] of dancer, building, audience.

I explore this notion of dwelling and hovering by giving myself time to *wander home* after rehearsal and I find a courtyard I have walked past a thousand times. But today, I am attempting to be incomplete, to be open to presence and hear it manifest. It unpicked itself from the rhythm of my normal march to the train station and called out to me, a circular soft space. As I turn to walk into it, I notice my breathing has slowed. A new rhythm I have missed many times before because I had a closed single relationship with this part of the city, the route-to-train relationship of almost out of breath walking-to-get-home.

> We talk about designing space, and that can have an intangible quality, which is the atmosphere of the lighting, the air-flow, and people can be changed by that. But it is also about the materiality, and how can material somehow talk about or invite dwelling moments?
> (*Architect* **C. VASILIKOU,** *conversation July 2019*)

I conceive of my dance hovering using images of material things; for instance, how do I connect with the wall or floor? But choreographically, I work more with the intangible such as light, airflow, texture. I see dance as exploring the incompleteness of the intangible by giving it the concrete form of the dancer's body: *Being* in the intangible of the perceived edges of things. As I dance, I find moments to dwell with what I had perceived as other, when I sense a reaching out to me from what I did not think I was.

As the *Being-in-Place* framework suggests the transaction of the situation, between things: texture, light, air on skin remind me of the possibility of edge while penetrating the spaces I move through. I/we wander the edges of perception when I linger, when I wonder what is around the corner, when I attentively notice the polyrhythms of *Place* and join them. I have hovered on and into *Place*, sometimes disappearing when the relationship I have with city is so unyielding that I can only be cast again, and again, as the same unknowable thing.

Dancing, I have memories of moments when the theatre stage, the lights, the music, have let me be semi-submerged in their 'edges' and together we have created something beyond ourselves. Some cities have merged with me too. In London, in Boston, in Lagos I become more than my Self – as city becomes me – and we weave ourselves across all the possibility of us. Or on vacation, leaving my hotel room in a city new to me, the anonymity of its newness gives me permission to be incomplete. I sigh in all facets of *here* that I can become. Or, turning a corner of the high street into a park, and as Andrew described, having a moment to remove myself from the relationship imposed on me (for instance, Andrew's homeless relationship with the city) and to breathe in the rhythm of the trees.

> I can dwell in this library and its quiet – or on my way home, there's a little park there and occasionally I have to make a call to my parents, and I'll just sit there for a while and make a call because it's nice and quiet before the hurly burly of home. So, I would say designing those kinds of places, where people can have that moment with themselves, or with one other person, or with your cup of coffee or whatever, is . . . and more and more to me, the really successful places are places that are rich in spaces where people, according to their little likes and dislikes, can have those punctuations in their daily routine. If you have none of that, then life is really boring and your environment isn't very rich . . .
>
> I think you can wander with greater abandon if there's some degree of orientation, the oldest one being the position of the sun, naturally. Which is why cities with an acropolis or a really tall building, a church tower or something, are so great because wherever you are, you can turn yourself around and sort of roughly know where you're headed. And I think [wandering] it should be accessible to everyone. I mean we all lead busy lives, whether you're a busy and wealthy business tycoon or a school

mum, we all lead insanely busy lives, but I think your environment needs to allow you space to wander, even if it's just for five minutes. Even if it means you have to wake up at 5am or just take a slightly longer route to where you're going. I don't like the idea of wandering being a luxury.

(Urban designer **S. PARTHASARATHY,** conversation August 2019)

To be with something is to be somewhere in and on the edges of where you and I meet. In and out of the blur between Self and other, flesh and brick. The situation, *Place*, becomes the awareness of being in community with [. . .].

Landscapes of opportunity

I bring two big bags of small stones to rehearsal. The stones are small, the size of strawberries. We are playing with two ideas. The first is creating metre-square spaces of textured floor to dance on. I line three shallow trays with different surfaces – a square of turf, a square of asphalt like grass and the small stones. I was expecting the sensation of the surfaces on our feet to be the primary instigator of movement as we play and improvise in the square spaces, but I find it is sound that leads the movement. Responding to the sound our movement makes on the different surfaces informs the movement. The stones are particularly responsive making a range of sounds as they move against the tray, each other and our feet.

In order to experiment further with the sound of the stones we remove them from the tray and place them in small piles. As we dance through the stones they scatter, tumble, skid across the dance studio floor and then come to rest. The chattering sound they make as they journey across the studio becomes a sonic illustration of the movements, we make to move them. A slide of my foot in a half-circular sweep sends dozens of small stones babbling across the floor in a fan of activity, extending my leg, my foot beyond my flesh. And then, within the commitment of each stone's journey there is a stillness and silence as the energy of my kick ends in the stones' motionlessness. Without the restriction of the metre square we can interact with the stones with more than just our feet. Through several twenty- to thirty-minute improvisations, we explore how the stones extend our limbs, our movements and our breath as we dance in and through them. There is an improvisation where we begin to adorn arranged stones on our bodies allowing them to drop as we move; we explore how ridges of stones are created as larger parts of our bodies slide push into them. My back pushes into a pile of stones creating an imprint of curves of my body. Stones respond to our movements, each individually speaking, running beyond us through the rhythmic energy our movement generates in them – sometimes scattering away from our flesh, sometimes hitting into us from another direction, sometimes stone and flesh settling onto each other. The stones and floor become the unanticipated extension of us, the polyrhythms of us brought to sound by our relationship with the stones – we are in community with them. The dance is the community of us, stone and flesh colliding with each other, riding the connection of energy, the sound of movement tracked by the scuttle of the stone, our breath, the squeak and thud of our skin on the studio floor, the possibility that is created between us.

In the stone dances, floor, stones, flesh, breath create sound, imprint, movement, rhythmic distribution of energy. Together, each becomes an extension of the impact of us; we change relationship again and again – a community in moments of moving and resting together. Hovering at the edges of each other, we are in community because the ownership of the dance, the movement, the rhythms is interchanged between the elements of the dancer, floor, stones. Jake Alexander records the rehearsal to devise the sounds into a composition (see Figure 12 – QR code link to film *A Touch*, that features some of this soundtrack).

As my arm shifts a group of stones sing out; most come to rest within seconds, a few steps away from me, but some find the length of the studio and continue the chuckling clutter of their rolling long after the silence of the rest. Joined by the rhythm of arm-stone-length of room is the sound of my next step on the floor as the motion of my arm pulls me off balance to catch myself in a lunge. The rhythm of six more stones responding to another dancer's curved sweep of the leg echoes my earlier arm movement. Arm-stone-length of room, step into lunge breath, leg-curve-six-stones all overlap in rhythmic responses. The extension beyond us that the stones sound and shape when they respond to contact with us offers movement that is at once generated from us and at the same time beyond us, creating multiple rhythms from the adaptations of direction and speed that is the sum of us, room and stones in dance. Community becomes the ability to join in with (or have present) multiple rhythms, responding to multiple moments and interactions.

I am framing *dwelling* as wandering the *hover* at the edges of Self and environment, being open to respond to any of the multiple rhythms around us. We found modes of wandering in the dance studio through seeing improvisation as a technique for responding to, creating and witnessing the polyrhythms of being together in any given moment.

> When I think of wandering, I think of exploring and I think of maybe fun situations and those kind of ways of exploring and interrogating a city. . . . It's an interesting thing when you start to put it alongside the term choreography or to choreograph, because I guess the Situationist movement in the middle of the twentieth century, for instance Guy Debord, were deploying games in sets of rules that they applied at random offence to choreograph their explorations. They were wanderings but they were wanderings to explore the city and to find out more about the city; to leave yourself exposed to fresh new readings beyond the kind of standard of operating within these set criteria rules. So, every time you saw the colour red in any kind of indication in the environment, you had to turn left. Or on the count of ten, perhaps the area you had to change modes of transport or the random sort of scenery. This gave you a way of wandering. So, your purpose is not a simple journey – where you go to work or go to school or are dropping off somebody or whatever – but it's determined by the other things. Those rules almost act like a tool for choreography or to choreograph the wander.
>
> (Architect/educator **K. TROMMLER,**
> conversation June 2019)

From studio stone-dancing to situationist walks through the city, movement improvisation seems to be used as part of the exploration of response. I am suggesting response and movement improvisation is the ability to see multiple possibilities, or rhythms, existing as choices to move between. Community is therefore the container that allows the acknowledgement of multiple rhythms being present at once. Choreographers and designers are looking for ways to slip between, hover through, the polyrhythm of *Place*. For me, part of the choreographic process is creating planned opportunities for moving between the extended rhythms that are the dancers, site and music. Choreographing becomes the act of creating a landscape of movement and the possibilities that are chosen to become the themes and motifs of the architecture of the dance.

> [It is interesting you bring this up, Adesola] as architects we have this deterministic approach. Thinking about starting from the lingering, dwelling part of space, to my mind, opens up a completely different opportunity, of exploring what we, architects, like to call the user scenario. There are all these studies about 'a day in the life of', kind of diagrams

we use, and we code, and we transcribe the imagined lifestyle and the narrative around the person, the specific user we are designing for. . . . At the same time, I am not sure whether, as designers, we have a lot of in-depth understanding of analyzing that dwelling part: What is happening? We use axiomatic tricks and three-dimensional views, or fly ins, or little videos, to kind of depict how you spend an hour in a very specific space. But again, that is driven by functional movement, the fact that one needs to sleep, wants to work, eat, the aspect of lingering, or paying attention to space around you being intrigued by specific aspects of, or trying to discover it in new ways or re-design it to feed a sort of specific purpose you have during the day, it is not really captured. So, I am feeling that these are the moments that we can start to include for that dwelling part that you mentioned, Adesola. There is a lovely example from John Hejduk, an architect that worked with experimental spaces, such as the Wall House. The interesting part of this was that the architect designed the sequence of a house, a series of spaces, into very, very distant sections of different experiences, and different movements. So, the space would really dictate a very specific movement. A corridor, a very thick wall that one had to stop to be able to have views of the outside. So, there was this change of rhythm, of movement, of stopping, pausing and going, that was instigated only by the shape of spaces and the way these were sequenced one after the other.

(Architect **C. VASILIKOU,** *in conversation interview, July 2019*)

From the stone dances, I consider how design indicates the possible rhythms you can make, movement interrupted and explored in order to make multiple opportunities of *present* available. This is not just to meet the aesthetic needs of different people. It is to suggest that multiple rhythms offer multiple ways to be present, to be at the periphery of oneself, hovering at the surfaces of 'we', 'us', 'community'. To have the availability of your full Self across time to offer the relationship of now.

Remembering stone dances

Whisper your name into the stones,
So that the tempo of these bricks crack.

Throw your breath at the sky,
That the vibration of your presence trembles buildings.

Then if you shatter into a thousand pieces,
Each fragment will recollect the assemblage of *us*.

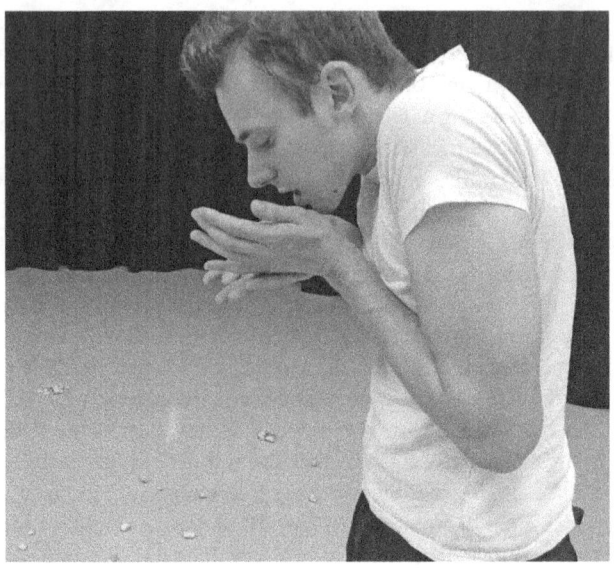

FIGURE 9 H. Fulleylove during stones improvisation and exploration rehearsal, July 2019. Photo A. Akinleye.

Performance of Self as architecture

Beyond Buildings: Performance as Architecture was an event I presented at in May 2019. The event was at the Royal Academy of Arts as part of Architecture Awards Week. Sitting in the Benjamin West Lecture Theatre – which was once an operating theatre – I worry about how my ideas of the city and the body will be dissected by the people coming to the lecture. I am speaking on a panel. If I stand up and talk, I feel I will be dissecting dance in the same way the bodies were dissected here 200 years ago; cutting into the flesh of dance with words while the audience looks on. I wonder how many women's bodies were dissected here, how their inner beings might have been hauled out and looked at. I wonder if my ideas about dancing and the city will be dissected with care or will be sprawled out on the floor of the static of verbal description. However, I was attracted to speaking here because when I was asked, it was said they were 'looking for more innovative ways to present ideas'. The hosts of the panel were excited to see if the space could be used differently and really wanted to incorporate the extra-large size of the projection area. Responding to this, I had asked to come and see the space when I accepted the invitation to speak. Alongside the encouragement to be *different* and a need to maintain the principles of not locking ideas solely in words, I decided I must dance. I must consider how to present a 'movement paper'.

To do this I pre-recorded the words of the paper I wanted to present as a soundtrack and developed a set of movements I wanted to express using the lines and shadows of the lecture space. I brought the *Isadora* programme to film me moving in real time and fed it into the extra-large lecture projector behind me. The *Isadora* programme was set up to capture only the images of me moving live that had come from me being still for a moment, the rest of the movement became a blur in the projection. The blur illustrated ideas around me merging, fading into the architectural elements of the room, becoming a part of the floor or seats as I moved

FIGURE 10 A. Akinleye practicing before panel presentation (1), Royal Academy of Arts, 17 May 2019. Photo H. Fulleylove.

FIGURE 11 A. Akinleye practicing before panel presentation (1), Royal Academy of Arts, 17 May 2019. Photo H. Fulleylove.

into the hypervisibility of my stillness when I stopped. This means that as I dance with the recorded words and lecture space the projection behind me showed blurred movement with moments of clarity when I stopped. It was set to be a few seconds behind the live movement so that the stillness of my live dance had a slight echo in the projection. I took the half-circular design of the seats of the lecture hall as a moment of incompleteness, meaning that the design of the choreography with the projection joined into a full circle. My live female body movement attached to the metaphysical circle of an operating/dissecting space. As *Isadora* captured the stillness of the structures of the room and my dancing Self, we, lecture seats, floor, projection, words, history and Harry filming, we approached dwelling and the city in terms of its multiplicity.

I was also playing with the architecture of the space by being filmed from the most extreme side edge of the lecture seats while people watched more from the front and centre of the curve. Therefore, the camera, like each person, had a unique view. We are used to the perceptive centre view as normalizing the image even if we are seeing it from off-centre.

Having the camera (and, therefore, the projected image) coming from the side addressed the thread of normalization's debt within this work; the point that design (and dance) create (spatial) norms as much as they can challenge them. This meant the projection slightly reconfigured the audience's relationship with the space. I was hoping this would give a multidimensional experience that required the audience to question their spatial relationship with me – their view – while the delay in the projection addressed the temporal of when *now* was. This all the while the soundtrack of my words was talking about the city, requiring us to locate ourselves and each other in spatial terms of tempo.

First part of movement paper soundtrack

The performance of the dance of the city is understanding Self and others in spatial terms. Listen, where are you? The environment affects my construction of mySelf. Emplaced: the process of being shaped by the material world. As I interact with environment it is not possible to have a disembodied view, life becomes performed, conceived of through the rhythm of interaction.

Perception of environment makes environment into a *Place*. Individual perception of a *Place* is through the boundaries and horizons corporeality creates, these structure the geography of the Self and performance of identity, the logistics of *Being* here.

The dancer's movement shapes both the physical body and the space around them through which the dancer moves. The dancer and the building, *Place* define each other.

'Space becomes more than just a hole in which to kick or spin about; it evolves into an architecturally fluid companion'.[2]

Dance is at the points of interaction, the edges of form that are highlighted by blurred distinction with environment.

Dancing-Self vibrates across the moments of the architecture.

The second part of the movement paper involved Harry moving around me dancing with a small projector in his hands. He was projecting images onto me. At this point, all the lights were down so low that only the light of the small projector illuminated anything in the room. I was visible only in the projected images that were a series of textures from buildings.

As Harry and I moved around each other sometimes small parts of my body were illuminated while at other times it was my body plus floor or seats. This section of the movement paper involved my movement paper equivalent of verbal questions and answers: I invited those in the audience to come and move around each other in the situation of Harry with the light projection, myself, the recorded words playing again and me dancing. I was seeing questions about the experience of being present during the movement paper as being physically 'answered' by people coming and dancing in the space with us. The feeling of being in the space, the experience, as a way of illuminating the paper further – as a Q&A after a verbal paper can illuminate a paper further.

Second part of movement paper (presented twice with audience interaction the second time)

Being
In
Place,
the idea that space and body create each other's shape – is the choreography of dance. We are in, on and between the buildings that are the landmarks of our everyday lives. Performing Architecture, dance is the mind-full-body in environment: an embodied – emplaced, lived-experience.

Our embodied experiences are captured and acknowledged and become the imperative of living together.

The history of the people – the touch,
situation,
experiences,
and hopes
are etched into the architecture of the buildings they inhabit, curves in the stone, paths trod into troughs. The presence of [. . .]
creates the building and buildings are created around the histories and hopes of those who dwell there. Brick and muscle locate themselves in terms of each other.

The *Place* of *Being-in-Environment* indicates how it can be interacted with, design conducts the melody of that interaction

And then we perform our presence.

When one goes to a lecture, in general, a small amount of all the information is absorbed. I was aware much of the movement paper would not be absorbed but I suggest that different people absorb different elements. I also maintained that I am working from an embodied belief that I cheat the research and artwork if, in the sharing of it, I betray any attempt to acknowledge its somatic nature. But I wanted to create an experience that could be referenced within the memory of the attendee. This can be done in the same way we reference a few lines of words when we remember something that was said. So, I hoped parts of the experience would stay clear for those attending.

Some feedback was about how hard it was to concentrate on the words. I had wanted to work from within the multiple modes of communication of movement, image (sometimes including writing), sound (including words). When we watch a person stand and read a paper the embodied *Being* has the possibility of being receptive to all modes of communication. But the habit of concentration is focused on the commonly received method of spoken words. My movement paper idea is to underline that we can mislead ourselves into thinking we have a fuller understanding or absorption of information because of the habitual ignoring of a particular mode of communication. We become more literate in listening to words about movement than we do in watching movement about movement. However, in the tradition of a read paper, you can ask to have a copy and re-read it. I wanted to make the equivalent, so I decided to make a film of the paper using the *Isadora* programme. I used the film created when Harry and Lauren filmed me moving slowly in the middle of city traffic in the street along the side of the British Library, a nod to the side view the camera took during the lecture.[3]

[Film: *On Dwelling* 5 July 2019. Using text from a Royal Academy of Arts talk on 17 May 2019. See Figure 12. Hover a phone camera over QR code to be taken to link.]

FIGURE 12 Video link to compilation five research and development films, *On Dwelling*, *A Touch*, *Green Version*, *Map Version* and *Whenness*. Films: A. Akinleye. (Hover a phone camera over QR code to be taken to link.)

Hyper-invisibility

Hot July days and we have chosen to take the DancingStrong Movement Lab into the streets of London. I stand on the Golden Jubilee Bridge and film down at the street (Victoria Embankment) using the *Isadora* programme. Harry and Maga are dancing below on the street. At first, I use the programme in the same way I previously described at the side of the British Library, capturing only the slow or still movement. Later, I create a film using this footage with the soundtrack Jake Alexander has composed using the sound of the stones in rehearsal.

[Film: *A Touch*, from research and development rehearsal on hyper-invisibility at Golden Jubilee Bridge, London, 25 July 2019. See above Figure 12, hover a phone camera over QR code to be taken to the link.]

Then we play with using the programme in the opposite way used during the movement paper earlier. Now, only movement is captured (stillness disappears). Harry and Maga dance on the island between two roads. Filming them (see film link in Figure 12), I only capture the movement of this event. When they stop, they settle and disappear into the environment; when they move they add to the exchange of people crossing the road, the speeding cyclists cutting across paths, cars, buses, leaves when the breeze played in the trees. Filming dance like this it is clear when relationships manifested. Suddenly, Harry and Maga are in tune with a group of people moving to cross the road. Then the relationship shifts to the sprawl of a bus passing by. The film highlighted the different rhythms they intuitively played with as they danced and captured how these rhythms harmonized around them into many relationships. *Dwelling/wandering*, they were picking and choosing across the rhythms of the street and the relationships they revealed. The camera on them, their clear skill at moving and the summer's day all supported them in being accepted doing this. Some people stopped and watched and in their *stillness* they disappeared from the film!

[Video clip: *Green Version* from research and development rehearsal on hyper-invisibility at Golden Jubilee Bridge, London, 25 July 2019. See above Figure 12, hover a phone camera over QR code to be taken to the link.]

As we made the films Harry and Maga used the programme to alter when they fade into the background and when they are vibrant, clear and seen.

We played with different colours of capture by tracking their movement on maps imposed on to the live capture (see Figure 12). As we played, dancing then coming back up onto the bridge to have a drink of water and to look at what I had filmed, the dancers were sometimes surprised at how they looked in rhythm with things they had no awareness of. For instance, the moving leaves of the tree made a massive impact on the filmed image and changed the orientation of the dancers' movement when you watched the film back – but the dancers had been barely aware of the leaves. That relationship was minor compared to the importance of noticing the timing of a bus coming up to the traffic lights that they had been improvising with. We further explored this at a traffic island in Hendon using an overlay of the map of the same road rather than a colour (like the green used in the film *Green Version*).

[Video clip: *Map Version*, from research and development rehearsal on hyper-invisibility using maps at Watford Way A41, Hendon, 26 July 2019. See above Figure 12, hover a phone camera over QR code to be taken to the link.]

I reflect on how the dancers moved in and out of vision as they wandered across the rhythms of the environment. It seems one can be invisible to the connection with *Place* and because of this, when you do stop to connect, you become *hyper-invisible*. I theorize that *hyper-invisible* people are people who are objectified. Thus, who they are is 'invisibleized' but, at the same time, they stand out from the environment because they do not fit the norm. I am thinking of dif-abled[4] bodies, women in religious garb, black women's bodies and homeless bodies. The price of being hyper-invisible is a lack of access to stillness. I ask Andrew what he thinks of my idea of hyper-visibility.

Andrew: No, absolutely, and I take your example of women in burkas, and disabled people as well, you know? [You] don't look at that person, he's maybe had a limb amputated or whatever, [you] don't look at that lady who is struggling to walk . . . what I love about the Hare Krishnas is that they refuse to be invisible, they just walk along and they sing and they dance and they smile and, I mean, that was one of my ways of not being invisible too. I used to sit on my sleeping bag at [a tube train] station and I would sing, because they can't arrest you for singing [but you can be arrested for begging or vagrancy] and I would smile at people and [it] really confused people that you would be smiling when you would be sitting on a sleeping bag. I used to enjoy confusing them and, yeah, if you appear happy, and you engage with people – 'hello', 'good morning', 'how are you today' – people look at you like you're absolutely mad, they do! And then the first thing that pops into their head is A, 'is he mad?', or B, 'what does he want, what does he want?' And people used to walk past me and I'd say 'good evening', 'how are you', 'how was your day', and they'd say 'haven't got any change mate' and 'I'd say I wasn't asking for change, I was just wishing you a good day' and then that would really throw them. I really was, if people wanted to help out then obviously that helped but that wasn't my primary intention. I kind of created my own little sanctuary of good energy in that space in the underpass next to [the] station and it was hard, always starting every day would be hard because you would be worried that someone would come along and be horrible to you and then that would kill your good energy, so you would have to try and channel [it]. I'd sit in the park first and just channel peace and calm and then I would go there and after about five minutes if somebody just acknowledged you and just said hey –

Adesola: And singing?

Andrew: I was singing or cracking jokes.

Reflecting on the research and development with the films and Andrew's queering of spaces by wandering through identities in place, I think about Fanon's Negro on the train, and McKittrick's demonic ground: being seen or not being seen is a clear set of rights; the right to be visible in the city. But I start to think about a different kind of invisibility, one I call hyper-invisibility. This is when the main relationship you are perceived to have is something that does not vibrate with the rhythm of your identity. Because you are perceived to have this main relationship all rhythms, actions and other relationships are folded around and re-directed back to this perceived relationship you are in. A relationship you do not feel you own because you do not see yourself in it. You are invisible because you do not feel present in the manifestation of identity that is being 'invisiblized'. For instance, homeless people are invisiblized in the design of my local train station but 'homeless' is not their main identity (although it is a lived experience that consumes their time). Andrew described this, when singing man or 'giving out cakes man' was his intended identity in his relationship with the *Place* of the train station, but he kept being redirected into a 'person asking for money identity' despite the activity he was doing. The hyper-invisibility manifests when the relationship one feels one is in is invisible, but one presence is hyper-acknowledged. There is no contingency for who one can be, no choice of relationship, no ability to wander across the rhythms of *Place* and choose a relationship with what is around you. The relationship designed for you is determined even when you don't hear your own voice in the measure of that rhythm.

As a Black female dancer, I have experienced this – the expectation of what my body can be overtaking the reality of my movement. I am organized safely into a shape where I can be ignored. My hyper-visible Black dancing body disappears in the line of white women around me. The systems within dance and within the stages of urban design hyper-invisbilize; offering the expected relationships we must take on regardless of the multiple ways we can see ourselves connecting. How do we create permeable spaces that respond to engagement rather than dictate it?

A dance to be made: *Desire Lines*

My reflections on *Lingering in Dwelling/Residing in Wandering* form as choreography. My choreographic notes for making a piece called *Desire lines*, about *Lingering in Dwelling* and *Residing in Wandering*, are two poems and a technical performance structure. Choreographically, I think about the aim to create moments where the dancers and audience can wander into new perspectives; join the current of one rhythm, then slip into another, experience simultaneous layers that complete each other through their incompleteness.

The technical structure for performance

This creates a performance space that reaches beyond itself to the audience. Four lights are used – one in each corner (two blue and two orange, and when they spill onto each other they also create purple). Two projectors are needed, and each will need to be attached to its own *Isadora* programme. When you step into this space, your bodily presence creates multiple relationships through shadow, captured image, projected image, physical body. The choreography plays with the layering of relationships. In the centre of the performance space, three small piles of stones should be placed.

Poems for choreographic development

Desire Lines 2 (poem for dance)

The way we walk through the streets leaks into the future of the cities we construct,
Foretelling the possibilities of who we can move into being.

'As the city limits' the walls etch identities –
Belonging becomes entangled with the privilege of Being.
Being becomes entangled with the privilege of Belonging

The poetics of my body is a terrain of muscles, bone, sinew, resistance, and tolerance,
In community with the slices of 'otherness' we move through.

Navigations (poem for dance)

And she would make utterances that silently shook the buildings,
changed the sky,
pulled the air into the corners of her world.
Listen, Walk, Disappear.
Magic crisscrossed patterns of diasporic, classed, unspoken
vulnerability
her heart beat into histories.

The empty spaces her absents left revealed more than they concealed.
She was seemingly in place by being out of place.[5]
She says
'I have to change this town'
But the toll of that is to change
herself.

Finding the city,
meeting it head on
was her series of remapping,
Her exercises in displacement.
Shifting the margins to the centre –
Stopping
Un-weaving the terrain of 'controlled'
as if it was the soft sweet braids of her own hair.

[Video clip: *Whenness (with poem)*, documentation of a live performance on Zoom, Theatrum Mundi Fellowship event, 18 June 2020. See above Figure 12.]

PART THREE

Part One explored interconnectedness as an apparatus for understanding my *Being-in-Place* framework as a potential scaffold for the subsequent sections of the book. Part Two was made up of collections of essays, poems, choreography and dialogue drawn together through movement and verbal conversations across a year of events (2019). These were organized by two themes that emerged from the movement and verbal explorations: *Chasing Stillness* and *Lingering in Dwelling/Residing in Wandering*.

Part Three, this final part of the book, reflects concluding conversations to the project that took place across 2020. I gave the manuscript of Part One and Part Two of this book to four individuals in order for us to have four conversations based on ideas about the events and reflections discussed thus far. In Part Three, I take these four concluding conversations to summarize and indicate next steps for the creative process/research.

The art of infrastructure comes from conversations with Dr John Bingham-Hall, director of Theatrum Mundi.

Choreography as questioning the knowable comes from conversations with choreographer, author, founder of the Critical Response feedback process, and MacArthur Fellow, Liz Lerman.

Whenness comes from conversations with author and professor Richard Sennett OBE FBA FRSL.

I am going to try to be a choreographer in the world comes from conversations with artistic pioneer and award-winning choreographer for concert dance, theatre and film, Dianne McIntyre.

6 *THE ART OF INFRASTRUCTURE*: REFLECTION CONVERSATION WITH JOHN BINGHAM-HALL

We are sitting in the café area of the fifth floor of the Tate Modern in Bankside, London. The windows running the length of the café look out over the River Thames and beyond onto St. Paul's and North London. You can see the layers of building jigsaw-puzzled into the Roman, Elizabethan, Victorian streets. London grows before our eyes in the slow circular motion of a crane moving a pylon into place on the side of a new build. I love the location of the Tate Modern, a now affluent area in what was the bear-baiting dregs of London centuries ago. London seems to pick itself up and redesign itself daily from here. We sit with the draft version of this book between us on the table alongside our pot of tea. John begins the conversation:

John: 'Reading the draft, you are talking about the way in which selfness is produced in a set of transactional relationships with environment that inherently sanctions people as not "fixed". If the city can be open enough, then it can become a constant process of "becomings". The city can become infrastructure for responsive societies and new forms of solidarities between people.'

The art of infrastructure

The 'now-ness' of my dance is an invitation not to be complete but to be in process with [. . .]. The challenge I have noticed is to avoid thinking and working in artefacts, in whole finished things. But the study of how a building should be built or how an existing space is being used infers an end point, a finished condition that will be created or is being studied. This implies all the elements considered have some finished point – the people, too, around the building are finished, labelled. But in the *naming* of a thing we close the possibility of collaborating, co-creating (of conscious transaction). In dance, in architecture, in engineering, in urban studies – in the West – we are forever in danger of beginning by limiting ourselves in the name of clarification.

John: 'People are often understood categorically. Think of all the things foreclosed when you are described as working class or gay or white or Black.'

In naming you are defined by what you are *not* and what is left is given the boundary of *name*:

John: '. . . rather than understandings of you as an emergent thing derived from how you are now in this space, people are identified by a classification through a fixed set of cultural artefacts'

. . . and in so doing people become the building's artefacts.

What is needed for a fixed set of identities has been mapped out and the city has been folded around the anticipation of those named people and their predicted needs. In these folds this kind of city art/public art is used as a memorial nod to the past, a provisional acknowledgement of 'othernesses', rather than an engagement with the 'now-ness' experience of art as it brings you into the sensory of the moment (Dewey, 2005).

John: 'Yes, for instance, in the ways that public art and cultural strategies might try to respond to a past or existing culture in a place, or create a new one, by distilling it into fixed representations. Such as the ways that new commercial property developments will include street or building names or pieces of public art that "represent" the past of the place as a working or minority ethnic community.'

As the city develops, that which is built is so often designed for people who are constructed as closed, finished elements; the built's ability to reach out and co-create with people as they inhabit it is not accounted for, not manifested as part of the collection that is city.

We are discussing infrastructure as means to support the un-naming, un-finishing of ourselves and acknowledgement of the ever-modifying, responsive nature of the transactional lived experience: an infrastructural approach that offers processes for, and can manifest new processes of, *becoming*. The assemblage of *Place* makes its manifestation felt in the changing forms of public cultural expression as populations and individual people change over time. This is as opposed to designing a fixed 'habitat' for pre-imagined people to *enjoy* their given day-to-day activity. This is not suggesting the emergence of transaction is blocked in this kind of overly designed architectures, as all things are in transaction (for the *Being-in-Place* framework is suggesting the transaction of things is how the lived is experienced). However, it means that into the *situation* of transaction is added the experience of pushing against the folds of the city, the limitation of invisibility of some identities, or the antagonism of no perspective from beyond prominent vantage points, or the exhaustion of identity as a set of difficulties. As Dewey points out with the fear and window shade example, identities do not disappear but can be experienced within fear, harmlessness or happiness, etc. Dewey repeats across my reflections:

> The experience has changed; that is the thing experienced has changed – not that an unreality has given place to a reality, nor that some transcendental (unexperienced) Reality has changed, not that truth has changed, but just and only the concrete reality experienced has changed.
>
> (**DEWEY,** 1977, p. 169)

Therefore, we could consider that if the city is designed for a particular set of identities, a set of realities (a set of truths involved in naming people into type), it also creates a sense of 'un'realities. These *un*realities, of course, are still experienced in the city, as Dewey suggests – it just means that the transaction of city will include the work of negotiating the knowledges made into *un*realities by being outside the set of actualities city was designed for. The transaction of people with city therefore involves the *desire lines* of reconfiguration of Self and structure. Then there is a tension of soft, unforgiving, constant refiguring back to template, designed into the relationships between people and built environment.

Rather than starting with fixed identities, the interdisciplinary conversations we have had during the *Choreographing the City* project seem to suggest exploring the possibilities produced by moving with multiple relationships that is the assemblage of *Place*. Then the idea of city could begin to shift from being the structures of a geography to the infrastructures for engagement in a geography. John suggests city as infrastructure, or indeed an infrastructural approach to thinking about urban design. Infrastructure here is the art of a network of responsive pathways (rhythms and relationships), a set of tools with and through which to make new situations.

John: 'i.e. becoming. Thinking about designing "infrastructure" is about designing underlying conditions, on top of which people can build their own spaces and forms of expression, rather than fixing identities through providing "end results" of creative processes (for instance public art works, creative districts) that are targeted at particular sets of imagined users.'

Thinking back to Eric's *Citybody* conversation, the city is the connection, clustering and making of the neural pathways of the *body* of people/environment. This is seeing 'city' as a set of circumstances, or possibilities made imaginable by the coming together of the group of materialities that are the people and things of the environment – *Place*. City is how one is facilitated in *Being* rather than the built structure one would be in. John suggest this means continued consideration of the possibilities that urbanism engages with.

Ghosts and the unfinished

John: 'Urbanists are associated with being about architecture, but I do think it is important that urbanity involves noticing a combination of political environments, overlapping networks of communities and cultures, the multiplicity of simultaneous activities going on, different meanings (such as at different points of the day); exploring how the environment is approached and used.'

As we reflect, John and I are thinking about urbanism as the study of the systems that exist in order to enable things to happen. The study of the constant reconfiguring dance of becoming, into and out of structure. Thus, urbanism is the study of the material, contingent on its meaning within the multiplicity of the political, sensual, historical, aesthetic, etc. Urbanism as the study of how things and processes are connected becomes a statement against the (capitalist) idea of the product of finished, completed landscapes being the goal of urban creation. Urbanism becomes about the betweenness of the elements of *Place* – the study of the *geist*[1] that is the city.

John: 'An unfinished landscape is hard to market but can be easy to inhabit because it has space to fill the gaps through doing. If the infrastructure is in place – the social, economic, technological support structures that underpin our actions – then people have a solid basis from which to transform their living environment. This basis might not be visible in the way the city is imagined but it is felt in the way it is inhabited.'

To create a site-specific choreographic work, I spend time in a building learning its rhythms (when are people around? When I am in the way?), learning its corners and how my bodily presence there augments them; learning where people place their emotions (finding bathrooms, where people go when they feel lost, tea and coffee machine areas where people go for comfort). In these rhythms and relationships, I start to find the infrastructure of the *Place* to dance with. Infrastructure appears like a ghost for me to partner with.

I step into the choreography and attempt to be in dance; the nowness of this moment. I bring to it the history and anticipation of future that is my Self. Like Sarah Baartman, if all that is seen of me is the material composition of my moving body then my spirit is threatened, shackled, lost. As a Black female ballerina, I have experienced the demoralization of this – I must be more to you than an empty body shell – dance resides in the wholeness that is me. Cities conceived of only as configurations of material objects are also shackled spirits, as if the buildings cannot become who they are. If infrastructure is the neurology of the body of people/environment, it is as if they design of the city has left it numb.

John: 'We need to avoid trying to design in a language that is in a completely different register than that of the language people will actually use to be in that place. (Not just verbal language – but language of thinking and narrating meaning to themselves and family.) This work on cultural infrastructure is about understanding the conditions that provide the tools individual people need (small, affordable, adaptable workspaces and so on) to make and share new forms of cultural expression so that places do not become frozen in particular histories that are exclusive.'

Design that foresees how a building will be used as finite gives a building a death sentence – begins it by predicting how it will be finished. Then, built environments cannot be who they are made into by the relationships they have with the people who use them because their predetermined (infra) structure restricts how they can reach out and connect. I wonder at how buildings live on as the ghosts of the idea they were designed to give life to. Of course, we agree in terms of economics, safety, environment that you cannot design the unfinished, but what we are suggesting is that alongside attention to the material shape attention to the network of political, social, emotional manifests as infrastructures that allows the materiality of shaping space to become a responsiveness of *Place*. At the heart of the *Choreographing the City* project is the suggestion that the conversation between (such as people and city, dancers and architects) is in a multiplicity of languages. We need to develop the techniques of communication that allow people to have conversations across languages. Rather than being about a built city, urbanism becomes about how we communicate, collaborate, nurture the city.

The aesthetic of becoming

If we are to remain in *becoming* through the responsiveness of a *Being* in learning with the environment, then design needs to allow for the infrastructure of learning what the environment could be becoming. Urban design would be aimed at living within the learning of *to be-in-this-environment* rather than design that is about making spaces to populate.

John: '. . . we need to be moving away from large glass-fronted buildings that are design primarily for one use. I am thinking of Rye Lane, all the different cultural practices of commerce that are supported in the design of the shops there. All the shop units are very simple, brick skins basically, they are incomplete – they have not been overly determined so that there can be a cultural process of becoming with a place, where changes or flows of people can be reflected within the environment. Whereas if the environment is too complete itself there is a decrease of the right to the city, the right to reshape the built environment as a reflection of your own cultural or personal practices.'

John's comments make me think about the *right* to be a part of the aesthetic of the environment you move through. As a choreographer, I create work that extends or complements but always aims to impact on the aesthetic experience of the people and spaces of the event where my work is performed. From this embodied perspective, the implications of the aesthetic of a building are important because it is a part of the outreaching tentacles of the environment that are engaged with in the immediacy of the senses. While choreographing, I am playing with aesthetics, reaching out beyond the dance to share a visual and physical connection with audience. In site-specific/public dance works outside the theatre, this is particularly relevant as the people who witness the dance being performed become part of the new history of dance having been present 'here', which changes their experience of that *Place* from then on. Dewey points out that art instigates a whole experience, in part because of its engagement with aesthetic (Dewey, 2005). This allows the person to be fully present in the immediate sensation of embodiment. The vitality of this supports linking to meaning and reflective thought in the continuum of their past experiences. The aesthetic level of engagement with life describes the quality of the embodied experience in terms of a lived connection with 'the world around', a vitality within the transaction of embodiment that is sparked by the punctum of an aesthetic. But this is more than just a pleasant experience of *helping to make something*; this is about the building blocks for how the city environment is available in a meaningful manner (a manner that connects with the elements of the identities of the people who populate it). That is the strength of connection that raises the act of transaction from the passive presence of the citizen in *Place* to the power of transformation within the transactional awareness of being a part of it all.

In July, coming back from dancing near Jubilee Bridge, Maga, Harry and I see some big concrete spheres on the wide pavement of the street running up from Embankment to Charing Cross. I start to get the camera tripod out and Harry and Maga begin to move towards the spheres in order to dance with them. A security guard comes over to us almost immediately and says, 'you can't do that here'. I ask if can we just film something, and the security guard glances up at the building's security camera – filming him speaking to us – and says, 'no you have to move on, I will give you a moment to pack-up'. He walks off to stop someone else from sitting on a sphere while I put the tripod away. As I am zipping up my bag, he comes back and says, 'thank you, it's a nightmare – everyone wants to sit on them or take photos or film, I don't know what the architect was thinking. But once I have spoken to you' – he indicates to the camera with his eyes involuntarily – 'you have to go, or I get into trouble'. As we walk away I think about all the architects I have been talking to and how happy they would be if their designs were being interacted with and how horrified they would be if someone's livelihood was determined by how well they could stop people engaging with the building that had been designed.

Taking my work (which is the aesthetic of the dance art I have created) out of the theatre to buildings and streets, it is noticeable that security guards, cleaners and caretakers correct things to the aesthetic they are being paid to monitor, which becomes the baseline of what the city should look like. This baseline is informed by their *Logic of Place* as adult people employed to stop it from changing. The security guards become the curators of the city's expected use. Aesthetic voice is neutralized back to the original design brief, regardless of if it was conceived for what could only then be an imagined population.

John: 'Incompleteness is a real political issue. Because completeness is used to fix and impose and control, where incompleteness has within it the right to self-determination.'

The marked lack of ability to formally impact aesthetically on the environment strikes me as a poverty, and links with monetary poverty. It has the potential to leave people disadvantaged in terms of the quality of their engagement with their environment in general. In the city and in dance culture, dance art events can be complicit by providing a tokenistic aesthetic authority. Communities of people who have little aesthetic authority over their own environments are often targeted populations for community dance arts and performance events, but any permanence or effect on the aesthetic of the infrastructure of the city (how it can be engaged with) is far from the reaches of the site-specific art and the community who has engaged with it.

John: 'There is a parallel danger that incompleteness can be used as a pretext for the withdrawal of the state as a shared support structure, a situation in which the strongest prevail and those in need of support sink further. This is why I find the idea of infrastructure so helpful. It is not a fixed concept, but I think it can be attached to approaches to design that enable and support without foreclosing on the realm of identity and cultural expression in the way that overly designed architectures often do.'

Similarly, dance performance can be inaccessible to many audiences, rupture its potential on expensive theatres stages or unload its relevance to the highest production value in competitions on television. Choreographically, I am excited by the idea of creating dance as an infrastructure to engage with something. It begins to inform how I could develop the structured improvisations techniques I have been using as movement conversations into participatory performances – public performance that is a conversation between building, dancers and audience. John is excited about the idea that urbanism must challenge itself to never be completely definable. John and I are concluding that the challenge to urban design and choreography is how we create infrastructure that actively includes participation. Infrastructure as the collaboration and co-creation of *Being-in-Place*.

7 *CHOREOGRAPHY AS QUESTIONING THE KNOWABLE*: REFLECTION CONVERSATION WITH LIZ LERMAN

My conversation with Liz Lerman about the manuscript of this book was divided into two Skype sessions.

For my first Skype[1] conversation with Liz Lerman, I am sitting in the Boston Public Library. I am in the corner of the more modern part of the building, at one of the tables that spill out of the café area. I had arrived at the colourful orange table I am sitting at by entering the older part of the building off Copley Square. This allowed me to look at the murals adorning the walls of the building, dating from 1848, then walk through the open courtyard in the centre of the complex. I then walked through to the newer part of the building. All this time, I was passing by folk studiously on their laptops, people reading – who I assume are homeless or have nowhere to go during the day – visitors to the architecture of the building and the exhibits, all smelling the perfumes of the books, eating snacks, using the bathrooms and sharing the building together. I am inspired by how people with what appear to be such different lives are brought together in the purpose of the library building.

The new part of the building has a reception desk opposite entrance doors that reads 'Free To All' lit in neon colours. I love that I can sit in the coffee shop area yet eat my own homemade sandwiches; and look at the ornate artwork from the 1800s alongside the illustration-exhibit from children in a local twenty-firsty-century elementary school. I have a small table with my laptop open near an electrical outlet, so it stays charged. Behind me is the main thoroughfare of Boylston Street rushing by, in front of me is the soft open space of the coffee shop, new building entry area and then layers of books and people browsing. It is warm here on an otherwise cold February day. Earphones in to hear better, I click the Skype symbol and after a couple of rings Liz is smiling at me, saying, 'How are you, Adesola?' Liz, adept at feedback, makes me feel acutely interested in my own wondering. After my first conversation with Liz, I have a list of ideas I want to research before we talk again! The second call I make is from my London home office. This is to conclude our conversation. I sit at my desk in my dressing gown quite late in the evening on a Saturday. Liz appears on my computer screen, and the sound of her dogs barking in Arizona fills my room in London.

Liz: '[In the manuscript] you are talking about the difference between the environment as something I walk through versus, the environment as something in which I am co-creating every minute of it; as I am breathing its molecules and as I am in relationship with the person across the park and how that changes how I might be, how I might actually manifest in the world.'

Us-ness

Choreography is a mode of exploring the knowability of a *situation/Place*. Dance choreography is the creation of a spatial language that gives the artwork a momentary set of rhythms and relationships (principles) with which to explore. I have talked about rhythm and relationship across this book, informed by a simplified translation of *Tā/Vā* offered by scholarship drawn from a Tongan world view (such as Māhina, 2002, 2004). I have used the notion of rhythms and relationships as embodied principles for locating Self, to alleviate the use of the disembodied language of 'time' or 'space'. Time and space manifest as modes to measure the experience of something, whereas rhythm and relationship lend themselves to the felt, transaction experience of something (Dewey et al., 1989). In this way notions of rhythm and relationship offer more embodied, transactional frameworks for locating *us* in experience than the linearity of time and space. Of course, *Tā/Vā* is more complex than being a translation for

Western ideas. Therefore, across this book, I have only used rhythm and relationship as a process to move away from dualist mind–body divides and binaries. I used rhythm and relationship in explaining *Chasing Stillness* as about *Being* in multiple relationships outside the dominate rhythm of the design (of a building).

Lingering in Dwelling/Residing in Wandering is about meandering in and out of multiple rhythms outside the dominate relationship of the design (of a building).

However, rhythms and relationships should not start to be treated as a binary: they are not separate from each other – they are not either/or. Rather, they are spectrums of reference for the knowability of the multi-dimensional experience of *Being-in-Place*. The danger with processes like these, that attempt to acknowledge a shift in paradigm, is that we continue to use them in the way we would use the very ideas they are offering alternatives for. The avoidance of slipping into binaries is the importance of what Liz calls 'nimble thinking', to be able to nimbly hold more than one idea at a time. Nimble-ness is to avoid the *trade-off* of 'this' for 'that' through an ability to be aware of more than one element at a time: the importance of us-ness.

Liz: 'Your use of principles derived from exploring the rhythms and relationships of a moment/*Place* reminded me of the choreographic work[2] I have done informed by thinking about Heisenberg's Uncertainty Principle. To paraphrase his principle, if you measure the shape (position) of something, you will miss its momentum. If you measure its momentum, then you will not be able to get its shape. And there is something about what you are saying about the nature of stillness and lingering and wandering that made me think about that. What you are saying is that *Stillness* is not the same as shape. Your description of *Chasing Stillness* is almost shape and momentum in the same moment. It is not shape because shape is static and it is not momentum because there is an edge to it, *Chasing Stillness* has a pulse.'

Heisenberg's Uncertainly Principle[3] points out conjugate variables (or Fourier Pairs). I take this to mean that pairs are connected, so in the focus of measuring one you affect the other. That is that many categories of knowability cannot be measured simultaneously with other categories (Lindley, 2007). The embodied markers of knowability are not independent of each other, for instance from an embodied perspective, the knowability of space is affected by time and vice versa (which rhythm and relationship express). In this case, Liz is talking particularly about the conjugate variables of *position* (which in our dancer corruption of the idea we have referred to as 'shape') and *momentum*. To apply Liz's use of Heisenberg's Uncertainty Principle, I consider implications in my own practice by reflecting: as I choreograph, I am making movement(s). To think about the movement I am making in terms of its balance between shape and momentum allows me to describe the movement to the dancers executing it or describe it to the audience watching it through my body. Sometimes, I am in the feeling of position (shape): a kind of visual aesthetic is uppermost in the intent of the choreographed movement I am doing; it may even be that I have drawn on a gesture that captures the position of a socially or culturally familiar movement. Sometimes I draw on the dynamics of momentum: a kind of velocity is uppermost in the intention of the movement I am choreographing. It may be to hurl myself across the room in a big jump or to slowly raise my leg from the floor in a balance. The see-saw between the shape and momentum of the dance steps allows me to adjust the knowability of the movement, beyond the assemblage of sensations within my skin, as I explain it to the dancers I am choreographing with.

By positing, in this book, that a dominant rhythm makes multiple relationships hard to attain (*Chasing Stillness*), and a dominant relationship makes multiple rhythms hard to attain (*Lingering in Dwelling/Residing in Wandering*), I am not intending to make rhythm and relationship a binary pair. I am suggesting they are interconnected through the embodied experience. Moreover, the conversations I have had across the *Choreographing the City: as/at the city limits* project have pointed out the importance of resisting rhythms and relationships as either/or constructs within the design of the city. The conclusions of *Chasing Stillness* and *Lingering in Dwelling/Residing in Wandering* warn against an approach of 'to be me, I must lose my sense of you'; 'to hear this rhythm, I must ignore that rhythm'. *Chasing Stillness* and *Lingering in Dwelling/Residing in Wandering* are about the balance of more than one mode of locating the multi-layered experience of *Place*. They are about Liz's *nimble* ability to hold focus on more than one thing at a time.

The choreographic questions emerge:

- How do we avoid making conjugate variables (either/or) within our perception of us-ness?

- Is making (for the choreographer, architect or engineer) the manipulation and exploration of tracing ourselves in the Δ (uncertainty/universe/Great Mystery)?
- Is making (for the choreographer, architect or engineer) the development of contingent schema for marking our own knowability in the Δ (uncertainty/universe/Great Mystery)?

Sharing

Liz: 'I believe the language you use – *Chasing Stillness*, "possessing the ground", "wandering", "permeability" "hovering", "dwelling" – all of these offers something in movement across dance forms. I can imagine whole workshops just with this language.'

It is exciting that Liz has drawn out this point from the manuscript because my interest in the *Choreographing the City: as/at the city limits* project has been to explore a lexicon for movement that can inform across dance, architecture and engineering. Liz wonders if dance today is hungry for ways to work or communicate across dance forms beyond the codification they engrain in our bodies. She references the global popularity of the movement vocabulary/technique Gaga[4] as an example of allowing people to start within their own movement form and yet work together. This search outside the codified seems to be an impetus we see mirrored in colleagues from subjects beyond dance too. Furthermore, in dance departments of universities, it manifests as a response to decolonizing the mainstream aesthetic of dance.

Liz: 'At my university we are striving for what I call aesthetic equity. Not ballet and Western modern dance making room for a bit of "urban forms", but actually have equity – which means the floors have to change, the context courses have to change and the learning outcomes have to accept and support these multiple aesthetics. With every innovation there is a sense of loss. It might be ballet, or jazz or even some forms of dance composition or improvisation. But as curriculums evolve the language you offer in the book can cut across all of that codification. You can have people in the room with all those skills – in fact, it might be a way those people can come together in the understanding of movement, not just trying to fuse forms.'

Adesola: 'Yes, rather than the treadmill of one practise replacing another, there is also a place for a language about the connection across dance within different dance forms. So, we are not just in a debate about "Hip-Hop in, ballet out," "no time for African diasporic dance because we have to have a quota of Cunningham classes" (or the equivalent conversation in architecture or engineering departments).'

Liz talks about the potential isolation of various university departments in and out of dance.

Liz: 'The dance academy is desperate for real connections across movement disciplines. I mean real ones not momentary ones. . . . I might have been dismissive of the Academy before I became a member of it. Jawole Willa Jo Zollar from Urban Bush Women has been teaching me this, what we are seeing is that the young people coming up through the dance academy are the people who are going to be populating the stage and people's companies (I mean, yes, there are people who don't go to school but a lot of them will have come through the Academy) and what are they getting, what are they getting?'

Adesola: 'Instead of spending too much time on the alchemy of the perfect curriculum timetable, we can also be teaching and looking at movement knowledges derived from artists sharing with each other from different forms and disciplines.'

Liz: 'Yes, [we can look at] what languages we need to communicate across these experiences, not for the emergence of a kind of fusion but for the ability to be "nimble" in our understanding – to hold two or more approaches within us at the same time.'

Liz and I are imagining a workshop where people from different dance forms come together and explore 'permeability' or *Chasing Stillness* etc . . . within their own dance form and then share that exploration physically with their peers in the workshop in order to share inside each other's practices (in terms of intent, world view, philosophy of movement – not just aesthetic shape). Liz starts to talk about planning our imagined workshop using the language of this book.

Liz: 'You can do action grids, so you have two axis and along one is everything you have been saying, the language of this book and then down the side of the other axis are different dance forms. Then you would not necessarily have to be a ballet dancer who becomes a hip-hop dancer to understand something, you can have all those people with different philosophical and contextual and original beginnings moving to the same "hovering" problem, the same "dwelling" problem.'

We agree that by seeing the process of a dancer from another form responding one could better understand the dance form itself in your own body.

Liz: 'It is possible by *Chasing Stillness*, for instance, a ballet dancer found their way to hip-hop more easily, but that is not the goal of course.'

I am interested in how research and creative collaboration between choreographic and spatial practices in architecture and engineering can help create new techniques, lexicons and ways of consulting with community around urban design and around choreographic endeavours. I continue to look at how choreography (seeing movement as a three-dimensional grammar) can contribute to larger discussions across subject areas. I feel the workshop Liz and I are dreaming up is a kind of dance *Petichta* (a special form of Talmudic scholarship that Liz talks about in *Hiking the Horizontal*) (Lerman, 2011, p. 215). The language of *Chasing Stillness*, 'permeability', 'hovering', etc. is taking non-codified dance notions (in traditional *Petichta* this is the equivalent of non-Torah, for example Psalms or Proverbs, sections of the Bible) and finding their connection with the bodies of dancers codified by their techniques (in traditional *Petichta* with a Torah verse). Finding the relationship between the two things newly reveals both their meanings.

Talking together, Liz and I are grounding the workshop for dancers in the practicality of how it would run. I muse that it could lead to interesting movement explorations working with dancers from across a spectrum of backgrounds. Liz says enthusiastically, 'I would do that workshop!' From my own artistic interests in movement making, I begin to get excited at the prospect of facilitating such an event but there are larger implications here within the dance community. The Dance Academy, the university dance department, has the dilemma of seeing training in one dance form remove another from the curriculum. This speaks again to how we avoid an either/or scenario as we create community within dance and beyond dance. This seems to be resonant in other university departments (architecture and engineering, for instance) as one process or technique becomes popular and merely replaces another. In my own reflection, I return to the idea that organization of training into subject areas could be augmented by stronger support for gathering communities of interest which cut across traditional divisions of practice. The dancers, architects and engineers I have shared conversations with across this project have become a community of practice through their shared interest in the shaping, politics, liberation and conception of *Place*.

Liz: 'When I think about community, I think about supporting communities that have chosen to be themselves. Like [instances where people say] "I am just going to be with the Jewish community," "I am just going to be with the Trans community." But then there is another kind of community building which is when we cross all of that. It strikes me that what you are doing here with this book is about a place for the latter. And that is harder to find these days. . . . I did a project with Bob (Robert) Putnam (2000), [where] he speaks about this. There is bonding social capital when you want to be with your own, but there is also bridging social capital – crossing boundaries. They are both important.'[5]

The choreographic questions emerge:

- How do we connect and become attentive to our practices beyond the codified routes used to first understand what the practice 'should' be?
- How do we have a focus on teaching dance or architecture or engineering, not just a rearranging of what forms/techniques will be most dominant?
- How do we make each other knowable through nimbly sharing the many moving rhythms and relationships of us-ness?

8 *WHENNESS*: REFLECTION CONVERSATION WITH RICHARD SENNETT

Richard and I are self-isolating in our respective homes during the March and April 2020 period of absence, stillness, hiatus of COVID-19. New recommendations about physically connecting with people have created an unexpected pause in the plans I had this weekend, and then this week, and then this month and then across this spring. The city is silent at times when it was awash with sound and movement. The streets and the people who usually occupy them are still. Andrew (just rehoused off the streets) has texted me saying 'and now for the Stillness you were talking about'. Richard and I are talking over Skype when we had hoped to be in the studio together. Richard has the manuscript of this book in his hand, and begins the conversation:

Richard: 'I love the impulse of this manuscript. . . . I had two questions that I wanted to ask you about . . .'

'Yes-it-is-made'

Richard: 'Where is the architecture in the manuscript? I see where the city is but I do not see where the architecture is?'

> **Adesola:** 'I see the architecture as the . . . – [*wordless I bring my hands together and start to knead the air in front of me between myself and the computer screen*] – . . . as the moulding of, casting of, shaping of the flesh of choreography, the brick of city.'

> *I think to myself – Richard's question leads me to consider how, at times, I have replaced the words 'urban design', with 'city', with 'architecture', and wonder if in the ideas I have discussed if have I put too little distance (along the spectrum of my own reflections) between the city as experience and the city as structure. I have been thinking of architecture as the knead-able, as the shaped, and in so doing I have been seeing architecture as both the activity of the choreographer and the activity of the designer.*

Richard: 'It's immobile?'

> *We are talking about buildings.*

In the Deweian landscape of my *Being-in-Place* framework 'no' built architecture is not immobile because everything is recreating itself in the dynamic, transactional reconfiguration experience offers. Buildings are slowly moving around us at hundreds-of-years-of-pace compared to the minute-to-minute pace of our human experience. But Richard is pointing out that our minute-by-minute experience is how we notice our lives – our achievements, our pleasures. (We feel things as ended or finished.)

Richard: '. . . but what about architecture as making something, what about the pleasure of "making some *thing*"?'

> *I think to myself – making something: completing, feeling we have finished things; when does doing the job of being an architect or engineer or choreographer end? The act of architectural activity as the practical response to a proposal. The challenge and satisfaction of making something that meets a brief and has reached a point where it is good enough to be produced.*

Richard: 'Do you have that moment in choreography? The gratification of knowing, okay it's good enough to be put into production, it's good enough to stand up?'

> *I reflect on how the moment of 'Yes – it is made'*
> *happens when I am choreographing. I have come to*
> *expect it three times.*

The first time *Yes-it-is-made* happens is during a rehearsal near the end of the devising process where everything seems to fit into place, artists are in flow with the concept of the movement and with each other. As a choreographer, I feel that is what I hoped for, the work has somehow found its own breath outside my inward envisioning. It appears to be here in front of me, beyond my skin. That rehearsal never repeats itself – the work is never that 'good' again. And for the other artists involved (such as scenographer, musicians, etc.) that moment might well happen for them during a different rehearsal.

The second time when *Yes-it-is-made* happens is at the first performance. This performance is rarely as good as the *Yes-it-is-made* rehearsal, but the work is completed because it has the element of audience – it is being witnessed – it is being interacted with as a work of art, not as a 'thing being made'. As a choreographer, it is only at this point I begin to have a full understanding of what the work is about – I glimpse it at the periphery of me and start to see the familiar of my/our making process as the strangeness of a new experience. Although I believe the art only begins its life through the interactions to come, the first time the choreography is 'aired' (through the move beyond the rehearsal studio to an audience) is a moment of completion. Often with little funding this might be the only time the work is shared and so the performance of a piece is often conflated with its finishing point.

The third time of *Yes–it-is-made* is during a performance a long time after the première. It is a point when the artists and I suddenly see the work as an entity of its own. Sometimes this is when a new artist replaces an original performer. The new artist 'learns' the work as if the choreography was something with its own existence beyond me, telling me, the choreographer, as if we are both learning the choreography together 'there is a jump here'. Or it is when the work has almost started to become mundane for the performers, because it has been done so many times, and suddenly a performance becomes an unexpected new experience for all, a new depth is found in the work and in doing so the piece steps into its own presence – a new life of its own.

I find each of these *Yes-it-is-made* points dangerous creatively, because I fear being satisfied with some 'thing made', that could be more; as Dewey puts it, the artist is striving to be 'always on the growing edge of things' (Dewey, 2005, p. 150). But Richard is pointing out that there is an emotional need to complete something, so it is *good enough to stand*. There are also financial implications, employability expectations and responsibility to complete something so that it is good enough to stand. These can be ignored; they are practical responsibilities.

The phrase 'good enough' (Ellsworth, 2005; Winnicott, 2005) is key in the transactional ontology I have been writing about in the *Being-in-Place* framework. 'Good enough' is the holding environment for some 'thing made' to bring forth or note a change in response. *Yes-it-is-made* when the response to it noticeably changes me/us; noticeably changes our understanding of our relationship with it from a relationship of making to a different relationship. I am suggesting that noticing a change in relation to some 'thing made' makes visible the continuity of having an experience with it. That change in relationship marks 'finishing points', marks points that something is 'good enough' to change relationship with you. The experience with it has changed from some *thing* being *made* to some *thing* else. These are points when the *made* can stand without us – a kind of birthing.

So, I feel the architecture is in the *birthing* of structures/buildings that others notice they can have a relationship with. Throughout this book, I have returned to the issue of how much we (the maker – choreographer, architect or engineer) can control what those relationships are. There are aspects of safety and usefulness that we control as part of the constitution of the thing being made. But choreographically, I cannot control what the piece will become in the hands of the new dancer, at the point repetition shifts the work into something else. There is a familiar moment when something is *finished* – but finished with the relationship *I* had with it, not finished by being fixed into a constant.

In the conversations with architects and engineers, there has been a tension between finishing something as fixing its use in order to indicate it is finished, and finishing something through realizing you have a marked change in relationship with it, allowing it to grow away from you.

Richard: 'For me, the whole pragmatist project is not about the success, about getting things done but about the interactions with others in dealing with resistance – that chapter in *Art as Experience* (Dewey, 2005) to me is so important as it underlines that if you don't have any resistance you don't have a medium to work in. I don't know how it is for a dancer, but I know for a musician that is absolutely physical. Even when we master a technical difficulty, the experience of struggling with it builds emotionally and is to do with release, how energy gets distributed when something is resistant, how tensing up impacts us – it must be the same for you. I just think it is so important in Dewey's work – it is not all plain sailing and I think that is what gives it a certain kind of gravity, a kind of emotional gravity, making is more compelling than just doing things with other people. It is that you are encountering something which is out of the terms of your just being together.'

One's lived experience expands as experiences connect with each other: as things come to finish points of *Yes-it-is-made* and reconfigure. Understanding is gained from a *continuity* as one experience adds to another. Within the meaning-making of our own experiences nothing is isolated; it is connected and develops into other experiences and knowledge. But to notice one is experiencing is the pulse and rhythm of expectation. In making, we are bringing together existing elements to reconstitute them into a different arrangement – this produces a resistance, as in a sense we are unmaking to remake. In making, we ride the current of expectation through the navigation of this resistance. There are points in that navigation when we notice the activity of making and finishing because of the struggle, opposition, surrender and expectation that foreruns our awareness of the transaction involved in the making. Therefore, the resistance, the difficultly of 'making', the awareness of sensation or emotion is key to being aware we are a part of the *Situation* of making.

In music and dance 'there is a rhythm of surrender and reflection' (Dewey, 2005, p. 150) in the physical attempt. Our awareness involves pause and rest and the notion of 'finished' is given context within a phrase, rather than through identifying an end point. Stillness and silence seem to become a part of the melody and phrasing of the dance steps or musical notes highlighting the resistance, the birthing and finishing and birthing.

Richard: 'I am talking about the maker's share in that, I've even had that as a musician – when [is it time] to stop rehearsing and just do it. It's not fixed in any form, but you say, "okay, enough, let's do it" – it's a kind of surrender too.'

> *I think to myself – it is like birth; you are giving something up. You are surrendering dominance and being alongside . . . I wonder, is stillness (as I have engaged with it in this book) a part of that surrender – to be with [. . .]? I feel from his point of view and as a musician, Richard is thinking about silence as part of this surrender too.*

Stillness and silence

Richard: 'I had another question for you – which is what is the relationship between *stillness* and silence? Because the arc of silence in music, from how long a pause lasts to a micro-hiatus, is such a complex issue. Often, when playing, rather than being at peace when you are silent, it is kind of ratcheting up the tension; [it is asking] what will happen after this? Whereas, at other times, it has that quality of stillness you have talked about, of inwardness. Last weekend, I heard a pianist friend play, there were moments when he would just bring the hands up off the keyboard and you know that this silence combined with that motion was a tension of "be-prepared-something-important-is-going-to-happen". It is just a microsecond: the micro-moments of silence, but they are anticipatory.'

> *I think to myself – for me, in dance, Richard is talking about that moment which feels like the cusp of the breath of the dancer. When the dancer's body is no longer anything separate from the space and time the bones are hanging in. Breath brings the 'outside' into the dancer's inner organs and the physics of movement carries them through the step as part of the quantum mechanics of the moment.*

Richard moves across the video screen as he brings his cello closer to the computer and starts to bow. I stand in my living room moving in socks on the hardwood floors between my sofa and fireplace: the COVID-19 self-isolation artist's studio. Richard is interested in the movements of his hand and bow which create the pause/stillness of silences encasing sound between phrases of music. When I dance to Richard's cello playing, I mark these by suspending my movement until I drop into the next step.

As I dance, the micro-pauses offer the audible 'betweeness' of the musical notes (sound moments of filled with silence). I start to turn, one, two, three times and then the slower turn four unwinds into five and disintegrates into the stillness of a turn-end, before I pulse into the fullness of the next step as the silence of suspension of the music meets me.

Or

an arabesque, opening my chest and upper back to lift my left leg behind and raising onto the tip of the toes of my right leg, hanging in the air in balance, breath out – empty stillness in the extension of myself into the space, I am suspended in the moment of equilibrium of silence, before gravity caresses my leg back down to earth and my weight cascades into the plie of the next musical note.

These moments of 'silence' Richard is talking about experiencing in music are embodied for me as movement (not stillness), movement marked by absence of intention. The end of the turn, the height of the balance are absent of new intention, absent of 'push', they ride the present. They feel beautiful because for the moments I embody them they ride the present with no hint at anticipation of future or crest on the refutation of the past (the 'end of turn' or 'end of balance' collapse time away from before and after). Those moments are the cusp of *now* – the absence of (linear) time. The intuition of time (and space) is replaced by the intuition of the sound/silence of the music. The dance that is Me steps out of time and implied in this is an agency that holds Me together to weave in and out of the movement/breath vacuum of change that is dance, whose cusps appear in momentary stillnesses or silences. We are not suggesting stillness and silence are the same thing.

Richard: 'To make any sound on the cello – the hand and bow has to be able to . . . [*Richard plays*]. There has to be a moment before there is actual contact with the string, which is a moment of silence in which you are already playing. There is a moment of silence before contact, and once there is contact there can be no silence.'

I move around my living room as Richard plays the cello trying to embody the points he makes in music.

> **Adesola:** 'There is a moment in the movement that takes over from the intention of what I am doing. Stopping of my intention and allowing of what is being, that happens in the silence.'

Richard: 'One thing we could look at is the way in which silence in music is the movement of the bow. The silence is not about absence of sound.'

> **Adesola:** 'Could we replace the word sound with intention, so we say silence (as we are playing with it now) is absence of pushing our intention? Allowing the moment before the next thing happens. It is hanging on incompleteness.'

We agree stillness and silence are not the same; in this conversation they are opposites on a spectrum. They appear as opposites on a spectrum in which *emptiness* sits in the middle between them.

Richard: 'So in other words what we are saying is silence is an activity (rather than the cessation of an activity).'

> *I think, stillness is also an activity.*

> **Adesola:** 'For me it is about unpicking what emptiness means. I feel as if we are saying silence is a sort of vacuum, awaiting the next – it gives you a vacuum into the next thing. It is a kind of premonition of *whenness*, not "emptiness" that has nothing of note in it but rather *empty* as without pre-fabrication.'

Richard: 'Well, that's interesting because now we could look at the relationship between absence and stillness. That absence is full of movement. The silence between the moment of bowing is not empty at all, it is very pregnant with something about to happen.'

For me, as a choreographer, stillness of the dancer is recognizable as pregnant with something happening: a period of summation of intention. As if intention was more visible in the still dancer about to move, than in the moving dancer. But the conversations across the project have revealed to me concepts of a *stillness* that is empty of pre-determined intention.[1] Before possibility, which involves the presumed allocation of intention, this could be what we are calling 'absence', 'stillness', because it is outside the assumption of progression (time) that intension must harness for something to become what it is intended to be.

From my movement perspective, this conversation with Richard has led me to consider a continuum that moves from silence to 'absences' to stillness. The agency of *I am* (. . .), this agency is the stillness I feel Andrew and Sowmyn discussed when they described connecting peacefully within the city. Not *stillness* as lack of movement or lack of sound or movement but *stillness* as an absence of a framework of time. Stepping out of the intuition of time into an intuition of connection: the moment we are a part of it all by being the pulse within. We return to the question of the multiple ways the architecture moves and is still that we began the conversation with when Richard asked, 'where is the architecture?'

I wonder at architecture responding to *stillness* as a marking of time (Eric's pause for a coffee because you are early for a meeting), and how architecture responds to another kind of *stillness*, as a stepping out of time (such as the central London park where Sowmyn goes to make a loving phone call). And all the embodied moments of *Being* we dance through between these are the hundreds of *stillnesses* that orchestrate movement. The architecture in this is in when the city, as experience, and the city, as structure, frame our ability to practise these range of *stillnesses*.

9 'I AM GOING TO TRY TO BE A CHOREOGRAPHER IN THE WORLD': REFLECTION CONVERSATION WITH DIANNE MCINTYRE

Dianne has built a legacy of creating choreography since 1972. She has collaborated throughout that time in concert with jazz musicians and poets, as well as choreographing for Broadway, West End and feature films such as *Beloved*. Each time we have talked, we have begun by talking about what is happening in the world around us and then, once grounded, we talk about the manuscript for this book which she has been reading over breakfast each day. Dianne talks to me on my home office computer via Zoom[1] from her house. I record our conversations. We speak three times and each time Dianne generously invites me into her world but also expects me to be brave, clear and precise. She is framed by the pale green walls of her kitchen with the rotating ceiling fan of her dining room gently offering pace behind her. We had postponed our first meeting because it was arranged for a time that ended up being when George Floyd's funeral took place. We both, independently, observed the service on live stream. When we talk the next day, we began by discussing the hope for healing we saw in the service and in the eulogies. The second time we arrange to talk, I am coming from a back-to-back meeting with a colleague about a mentoring legacy fund I am helping set up in remembrance of a prominent dancer in my community. We began with Dianne asking me about the starting the organization and how it is going. The final time we meet, Dianne is a few minutes late as she was finishing some emails for a project she is planning. She has been very busy confirming plans for projects that were initiated before spring 2020's COVID-19 lockdown. They are now being redreamed by her in response to the world we are all emerging into. Throughout our conversations, Dianne asks me questions to prompt me to better articulate sections of the book and after I have answered a question, she says 'I'm glad you are recording that – that was good'. I feel that process as if I were in the rehearsal studio with her, as she would ask me to do a step from a piece of choreography by prompting me about the intention or weight of the step and watches/listens while I explore the step again before letting me know when it strikes a chord, hits the note, finds its flow – 'that was good – keep that'.

I want to try to be in the world

Dianne and I have discussed how one claims one's creative practice – something that stems from a personal decision to try to be a choreographer (or architect, or engineer). And then, having made that claim, what is the responsibility one has to the creative process? Dianne is particularly interested in how Terry talks about being aware of what 'seeps' into the work one is making (during my conversation with him and Eric on waiting).

> After years and years [a] way of thinking seeps into who you are, and you can see how that perhaps seeps into the designs.
>
> **(TERRY,** *above page 56*)

We start to discuss a distinction between making/creating work that could become mechanical – reproducing a formula – juxtaposed with a sense of making/creating as something with attention to noticing what foundationalist ideas we have personally absorbed from the world around us. When Dianne speaks to me, I feel she is suggesting part of the responsibility of artists is to be conscious in the world, in dialogue with it, aware of how experience from across our whole life must shape our work to be in conversation with the time we live in.

Dianne: '. . . You make that choice; [you say] I am going to try to be a choreographer in the world.'

I breathe.

Dianne: 'I have a question, is the main point of this manuscript "otherness" in architecture and engineering in terms of how "otherness" is designed for? For instance, when you say on page 69, "Un-geographic, geography-less in part because of how difficult it is for non-white, queer, working-class, female, and non-mainstream bodies to have a spatial relationship with their surroundings that reflects their self-identity." Or, is the main point of the "otherness" about the "otherness" of dance when in collaboration across disciplines and environments such as when you were dancing on London Bridge in the busy pedestrian traffic?'

Adesola: 'Both: an important concern in this project is that there are some bodies that do not fit in the cities, or are even present in the history of the cities, they live in. That is a problem because the city is representing, here, the environment in which people interact and create society together. What I am saying is, what the suggestion is, is that the reoccurrence of these problems calls for continued exploration into different ways we can perceive/address them. Maybe if we come together and start to use each other's practices to explore – maybe we can help each other. So, by using the knowledges in dance – which is also about movement and space – maybe architects and engineers will see a problem differently or recognize it differently, where they don't seem to recognize it with the current tools that they have. When I was asked to be involved in the Theatrum Mundui project *Choreographing the City* the assumption was that the culture of dance could do that – and what I pointed out was that there are subjugations and exclusionary histories in dance also. It is not an issue that dance can come and save other things because we have our own problems. The *city* is not a subject-based issue (of architecture and engineering), the city seems to be an issue of where humanity is currently, in general – so maybe by coming together across practises we also can address these larger social issues that somehow our practices manage to keep marginalizing. In breaking the isolation of one practise verses another practise, we might also come across some things that help us resolve, help us heal in other places.'

Dianne ponders: 'How do you get trained [in Euro-America as a dancer, architect, engineer] and have [what Euro-America would call an] "other" consciousness inside that training?'

As we talk, Dianne reflects on the value of referring to architectural composition from non-Western cultures and wonders if that would be among some of the next steps indicated by the book. She goes on to draw out my points by asking me questions:

Dianne: 'Adesola, you speak about Black, female, queer, people with disabilities (dif-abled). How can the queer person be identified as "other" just by looking at them? Looking at the person of colour and the person with the disability (dif-abled) sometimes you can see they are different from a privileged, white male who is not living with a (so-called) disability?'

Adesola: '. . . Also working class, I include that categorization too. I think that none of these are necessarily indicated visually – you can't see all dif-abilities, and also with race, identification of race changes over time and in different geographic areas. I am suggesting that the design of cities can collude with some groups of people to make "others".'

Dianne: 'Hmm, I question social constructs that focus on pointing out "others." Is the study and conversation at this period on "other" necessary to get past it and to heal in some way? One is only "other" when made to feel like that way or when one's own self-view causes one to feel outside of the main focus. Because the "ruling" class makes it so? I do not like to be labelled "other." Does the majority make everyone else other? Years ago, I had my dance studio in Harlem in New York City. Every day, I saw mostly Black people. White people were often afraid to come to Harlem – I don't think because they thought it was dangerous so much as it was because since they labelled "otherness" in Harlem they would have felt *othered* themselves – in their own minds. Once when I visited a village of Pueblo-dwelling people in the south-western USA. I saw in the crowd a girl who was a Black female teen. She was also a Pueblo-dwelling, Indigenous girl. For my eyes, she was a Black girl in the midst of this community – however, for the community she was not "other" – she was of that community, a daughter. Community and who is of community? Community can be more expansive – that is the dream – and then there will be no othering.'

Adesola: 'Yes, the notion of "race" has been divined to conceptualize that *difference* is something that can primarily be seen. The effect of all prejudices (racial, gendered, sexual, economic) are oversimplified when it is reduced to a matter of making a space to have people of those groups literally standing in your line of vision. It does not address the environment that those people are having to endure in order to be seen. It underestimates the injustices of prejudices (of course, each of these categorizations I mention suffer different applications of injustice that create different outcomes – different issues and different pain) but none of them are just about being in sight, they are about being productively a part of it all. In terms of racism and misogyny, obviously most people can identify you by the colour of your skin or gender (although some people can "pass"). But I am talking about how it is much deeper kind of exclusion; it is a much deeper environmental absence of what one needs to grow.'

Dianne: 'Yes, I see what you are saying. It has only been a short time since there have been laws mandating all public buildings to be accessible to everyone. However, to design environments considering race, gender, sexuality, class, people with so-called disabilities (or dif-abilities) so that everyone can flourish in those environments, that is something that will take deep study and big shifts. I suppose it can start to happen when the fields of architecture, engineering and city planning are abundant with people now considered "other" whose studies go beyond the Euro-American paradigms and who can then revolutionize the field.'

Dianne continues: 'Also, about quiet space, that was very intriguing to me – for architecture and art. If cities were designed to have places just to be outside of one's house, apartment or dwelling – this would be a public place – not just to wait or to pass time when early for a meeting – this is a place to contemplate, be quiet, imagine, see trees and clouds and people. It is a place where artists can conjure. It is not a park where you have to go far away – it is present, close by. I liked the contemplations in the section on stillness and intention within stillness.'

Adesola: 'Overall, what I am saying is that, while things are made for the intention of a small mainstream group of people, while things are made for the intentions of white cis straight men, anyone else's intentions (whether you can tell they have them or not by what they look like) become fragile and that is a loss to the whole population.'

Dianne: 'Okay, that's clear. So, one thing I can't imagine because we live in the spaces that we live in, I don't know, I can't imagine what a space would be that would be different.'

Adesola: 'I think that it is important not to know, but to have an idea, a "seed" as you call it, Dianne. Not to fully know something before you have created is what artists are adept at. I feel at points of social consciousness in our histories, people have realized that what they thought was a reasonable fair reality is demonstrating that it is not. This is to do with the colonial notion of discovery – the assumption that when something is brought to your attention it is not just new to yourself but also new to the world. This is privilege – the privilege to "discover," the privilege to limit reality around your own awareness. The problem can be that then people try to get back to what the "beautiful world" was like before their *discovery* of the injustice. But in trying "to fix it" they are, on some level, attempting to get back to an episode of their own fiction. So, rather than get back to a preconceived idea, part of our task is to be making, creating, working toward the spontaneous composition of now – we have to have the courage, as artists are familiar with, to go into something with the awareness that as we interact with it we determine it. We are creating and exploring the world simultaneously.'

'Spontaneous composition'

Dianne says that my definition of dance/dancer/dance training (page 15) is important.

Dianne: 'You write that "a 'dancer' is anyone who can recognize the *situation* . . . of dance . . . This continuity of reflection drawn from the experience of dance begins to describe the artistry of dance . . . the individual who focuses on preparation for the circumstances of dance by fine-tuning reflective thought and muscular body in order to play with and manipulate and generate the *interaction of dance* is the 'professional dancer'/'trained dancer' . . . 'dance technique' prepares one for the *interaction of dance* and provides guidelines for the safe execution of movement along particular aesthetics"'.

Dianne has looked at this section with me to encourage me to be precise here. We discuss how some of the knowledges of dance and choreographing with dance are about the ability to be responsive. Part of this section is also about how we each (as dancers) construct what it is we are doing when we dance: there is something very personal about what dance can be to each person who claims they do it; this is because dance is not just a thing done, it is also a process of engagement with – a response to now. Therefore, each performance is not the same. In Dianne's work, part of the language of the movement is a response to the moment/music/environment. It is as if a piece is a different version each time it is performed because the sensibilities of the performers in the moment is what Dianne has asked of the movement. For me, this reflects Dewey's notion of *transaction* – the dance is alive because the choreography is the intersection of now with the intention of the steps. Dianne calls this responsiveness-improvisation in her work the element of *spontaneous composition*. She explains that because the word *composition* acknowledges and elevates what is happening in order to recognize, it is informed by the continuity of knowledges and preparedness for dance that the dancers possess; composed and yet responsive. I feel it is this same ability to be lively in spontaneous composition that we have all been talking around when we have discussed being in the *city*: city as spontaneous composition. In her work, Dianne has described wanting to achieve oneness between audience and dancer. Dianne describes for me what this means to be dancing, alive in nowness, in oneness.

Dianne: 'I was fascinated by your idea of the oneness related to the concepts in choreography and architecture, how they can borrow and learn from each other. How I see the oneness between the audience and the dance (I can see it more when I am performing – well, not just when I am performing, I can see it with people when they are performing too). It is a kind of . . . where you empty yourself (people might do this in different ways) you empty yourself so that what you are expressing is beyond you, your own body, your own mind, your own ego, (you know all your moves – even if you don't know them completely all that well) – you empty yourself so that the person or people who are experiencing what you have to offer, as a true offer and then they can connect with what your intention is, because you let down a kind of barrier that can be built up with ego, or with finesse of your technique, or of your worry ("Is this going to be ok?"), or of your whatever, or of your seeing yourself in the mirror. Those are barriers. When those barriers are dropped the audience can go inside of the intention of the work. And then sometimes when that happens their minds can be lit up, their hearts can be expanded, they themselves can be creative in whatever it is they do in their own lives – that for me is the purpose of dance, that is the purpose of art.'

We sit in silence together after Dianne has said that, we breathe the world together for a moment, and then . . .

NOTES

Glossary

1 Available at: https://www.nytimes.com/2014/11/19/opinion/the-case-for-black-with-a-capital-b.html

Part One

1 Theatrum Mundi Research Fellowship, phase one, 2019.

Chapter 1

1 McKittrick (2015).
2 Bourdieu (1990), Burkitt (1999), Foucault and Sheridan (1979), Gould (1996), Shilling (2005), and Synnott (1993).
3 This draws on Shannon Sullivan's description of somatic knowing before verbal language when she adopts Gendlin's (1992) use of '. . .' as an indicator of this in her book *Living Across and Through Skins: Transactional Bodies, Pragmatism and Feminism* (Sullivan, 2001).
4 Mitakuye Oyasin is a Lakota world view (and prayer) This translates to 'we are all related' or 'we are all connected' (New Lakota Dictionary, 2008).
5 Physical and verbal conversations.

Chapter 2

1 Whereas traditional preservation, in different guises, could be seen as occupying the centre ground of the notion of dancing.

2 For instance, Bharatha Natyam could be seen as classical/traditional in that it has a long history in which the dance has changed dating back to 300 BC (Meduri in Dils and Albright, 2001) and many people have impacted on how the dance is experienced today.

3 Movements of dance in one culture, which would of course have their own historical, aesthetic and geographical reference points, could not appear to be dance in another culture (Jonas, 1992; McFee, 1992).

4 For instance, Jingle Dress Dance could be seen as contemporary in that it has a history from beginning of 1900s, and we know the first person to dream/envision the dance steps (Garcia, 1991). However, as contemporized dance progresses through time/space, it moves from being contemporary to being classical/traditional as it is added to and executed by more and more people from differing times and geographic locations (individual movement exploration made by Martha Graham becoming the Martha Graham Technique now taught by a number of people worldwide).

5 These are my inferences, drawn from having practised and taught a range of dance techniques, as well as spoken to movement specialists, and the literature particularly of Merce Cunningham, Alwin Nikolais, Murray Louis and Julio Horvath.

6 For instance, in the past I have danced with children who were non-ambulatory and could barely move their muscles: they were exploring the sensation of dance through (tiny) considered movements for the sake of the movement itself. They defined what they were doing as dance in these circumstances and as I got used to how their bodies moved I could see the difference between their habitual movements and when they conveyed dancing with me.

7 However, it is also important to note many of those attending workshops identifying as architects and engineers also took regular evening classes in different kinds of movement practices (despite their reluctance to claim being able to dance!).

8 In a conversation with Dianne McIntyre about the manuscript she pointed out that choreographers sometime call what they are doing 'making up a dance' and also sometimes appear not to edit, as they come with a piece worked out internally before rehearsal. I am using the phrase 'making up dances' to represent a single dimensional act of stringing movement whereas I use the word choreography to represent a more multi-layered composition. Dianne's point is to remember that some choreographers' multi-layered compositional task is to pare back to a single dimensional act of movement!

9   Although many of those identifying as architects and engineers, and even some who said 'they don't dance', regularly took evening classes in dance or another movement practice.

10 Le Corbusier's love of dance is present in his photo essay 'Milestones' in *L'Espirt Nouveau Magazine*. He met and became close with Josephine Baker during the period when he designed Villa Savoye (Regensdorf, 2019; Wilson, 1996; Woodman, 2014). It is not the geographical location that makes something site-specific but the challenge of 'use' *of* (interaction with) the unique attributes of the environment to inform the creative and performance process.

11 I am using the word choreography very widely here – including seeing the technique movement sequences of a style of dance as choreography.

Chapter 3

1   A container that can then be used for verbal languages as well as non-verbal ones.

2   This is a pseudonym – used to acknowledge that some of the projects and bids that Terry works on are confidential.

3   My emphasis.

4   When a dancer stands on one leg and extends the other leg at hip level behind them.

5   On the contrary, it seems there is a lot of work about the questions of objectification of the body through dance.

6   Particularly within a democracy.

7   North-eastern Native American nations notion of welcome, community and acceptance of difference as adding to the greater good.

8   Likewise, Heidegger's work on *'dwelling'* and his 'fourfold' (earth, sky, divinities and mortals) (Sharr, 2007) suggests that the experience of a place constructs an individual's identity through creating circumstance for living. An individual's perception of their environment makes that environment into a *Place*. Individual perception of a place is through the boundaries and horizons they create; these structure the geography of the space as much as they structure the individual's identity. In his later work, Heidegger was very interested in how buildings and architecture could shape people through the experience of interacting with them (Heidegger, 1989, 2006; Sharr, 2007).

9   The place attributed to housing the mind.

Chapter 4

1. I only notice when they affect the structure of an organ-building too.
2. These are exciting opportunities for collaboration in terms of technologies coming together to create some artwork. But the goal of the conversations was to see what was in the unknown between our practices not what we could make by just putting them together.
3. *Inventory of Behaviours: Regulation, Resistance and Readiness* at the Tate Modern (Tate Exchange 5th floor) I spoke at this event on June 20th, 2019 which is on-going research being done by Jo Addison, Kingston University, London UK and Natasha Kidd, Bath Spa University, Bath UK.
4. All public toilets were made cost free in major rail stations in London from April 2019.
5. A live capture film and projection programme.

Chapter 5

1. Also Larry, who was present in earlier non-recorded conversations.
2. Nikolais and Louis (2005, p. 11).
3. The process of dancing in streets and how close cars would come to me on the edge of the pavement around the British Library taught me a new lesson in stillness and ownership of the ground that the original movement paper had not covered. I have discussed this in the *Possessing the Ground* section.
4. I am adopting the term 'differently-abled' bodies which I have shortened to 'dif-abled'. See also Glossary.
5. Sentence inspired by wording from McKittrick (2006).

Chapter 6

1. Hegel, Dyde and Ebrary (2001).

Chapter 7

1. An online video meeting platform.
2. Small Dances About Big Ideas, 2005.
3. $\Delta x \Delta p \geq \dfrac{h}{2}$.
4. Gaga was developed by Israeli artist Ohad Naharin, director of Batsheva Dance Company. Gaga students improvise movement based on their own somatic responses to imagery, description and intensions provided by the person leading the class in a real-time nature.
5. Putnam (2000).

Chapter 8

1. When I danced the slow sunrise dance on London Bridge, my presence lacked the assumed intension that the bridge was something to move across quickly.

Chapter 9

1. An online meeting platform that became popular during the spring 2020 COVID-19 global lockdown.

BIBLIOGRAPHY

Akinleye, A. (2012). 'Orientation for communication: Embodiment, and the language of dance'. *Empedocles: The European Journal for the Philosophy of Communication*, 4(2), pp. 101–12. DOI:10.1389/ejpc.4.2.101_1

Akinleye, A. (2019a). 'Play: "Ideas are statements not of what is or what has been but of acts to be performed"'. In J. Bacon, R. Hilton, P. Kramer and V. Midgelow (Eds), *Research (In/As) Motion: A Resource Collection, Artistic Doctorates in Europe*: Theatre Academy, University of the Arts Helsinki.

Akinleye, A. (2019b). '" . . . wind in my hair, I feel a part of everywhere . . .": Creating dance for young audiences narrates emplacement'. *Journal of Dance and Somatic Practices*, 11(1), pp. 39–47. DOI:10.1386/jdsp.11.1.39_1

Akinleye, A., and Kindred, H. (2018). 'In-the-between-ness: Decolonising and re-inhabiting our dance'. In A. Akinleye (Ed.), *Narratives in Black British Dance: Embodied Practices*, pp. 65–78. London: Palgrave MacMillan.

Allen, P. G. (1992). *The Sacred Hoop: Recovering the Feminine in American Indian Traditions: With a New Preface*. Boston: Beacon Press.

Anderson, K. (2000). *A Recognition of Being: Reconstructing Native Womanhood*. Toronto: Sumach Press.

Ballantyne, A. (2007). *Deleuze and Guattari for Architects*. London: Routledge.

Barthes, R. (1981). *Camera Lucida: Reflections on Photography* (R. Howard, Trans.). New York: Hill and Wang.

Beall, A. (2018). 'In China, Alibaba's data-hungry AI is controlling (and watching) cities'. *Wired*. Retrieved from https://www.wired.co.uk/article/alibaba-city-brain-artificial-intelligence-china-kuala-lumpur

Bernasconi, R. (Ed.) (2001). *Race*. Malden, MA and Oxford: Blackwell.

Bingham-Hall, J., and Cosgrave, E. (2019). 'Choreographing the city: Can dance practice unform the engineering of sustainable urban environments?' *Mobilities*, 14(2), pp. 188–203. DOI: 10.1080/17450101.2019.1567981

Black, E., and Neihardt, J. G. (1932). *Black Elk Speaks*. New York: W. Morrow & Company.

Black, H., and Jackson, D. (1990). *Black Hawk: An Autobiography* (Prairie state books edn). Urbana: University of Illinois Press.

Blanchot, M. (1993). *The Infinite Conversation*. Minneapolis: University of Minnesota Press.

Bourdieu, P., and Nice, R. (1990). *The Logic of Practice*. Cambridge: Polity.
Burkitt, I. (1999). *Bodies of Thought: Embodiment, Identity, and Modernity*. London; Thousand Oaks, CA: Sage Publications.
Butler, J. (1990). *Gender Trouble: Feminism and the Subversion of Identity*. New York and London: Routledge.
Casey, E. S. (2009). *Getting Back into Place: Toward a Renewed Understanding of the Place-World* (2nd edn). Bloomington: Indiana University Press.
Deleuze, G., and Guattari, F. (1983). *Anti-Oedipus: Capitalism and Schizophrenia*. London: Athlone.
Deleuze, G., and Guattari, F. (1987). *A Thousand Plateaus: Capitalism and Schizophrenia*. London: Athlone.
Dewey, J. (1958). *Experience and Nature*. New York: Dover Publications.
Dewey, J. (1977). *Dewey and His Critics: Essays from Journal of Philosophy* (S. Morgenbesser, Ed.). New York: Journal of Philosophy, Inc.
Dewey, J. (1997). *How We Think*. Mineola, NY: Dover Publications.
Dewey, J. (2005). *Art as Experience* (Paperback edn). New York: Penguin.
Dewey, J. (2007). *Human Nature and Conduct: An Introduction to Social Psychology*. New York: Cosimo.
Dewey, J. (2008). *Human nature and conduct* (New ed.). New York: Barnes & Noble.
Dewey, J., Boydston, J. A., and Toulmin, S. (1984). *John Dewey: The Later Works, 1925–1953* (Vol. 4: 1929, The Quest for Certainty). Carbondale: Southern Illinois University Press.
Dewey, J., Boydston, J. A., and Lavine, T. Z. (1989). *John Dewey: The Later Works, 1925–1953* (Vol. 16: 1949–1952, Essay, Typescripts, and Knowing and the Known). Carbondale: Southern Illinois University Press.
Dills, A., and Albright, A. C. (2001). *Moving History, Dancing Cultures: A Dance History Reader*. Middletown, CT: Wesleyan University Press.
Dreyfus, H. L., Rabinow, P., and Foucault, M. (1983). *Michel Foucault, Beyond Structuralism and Hermeneutics* (2nd edn). Chicago: University of Chicago Press.
DuBois, W. E. B. (1989). *The Souls of Black Folk* (Bantam Classic edn). New York: Bantam Books.
Dunbar, R. I. M. (2004). *Grooming, Gossip, and the Evolution of Language* (2nd edn). London: Faber.
Ellsworth, E. A. (2005). *Places of Learning: Media, Architecture, Pedagogy*. New York: RoutledgeFalmer.
Fanon, F. (2008). *Black Skin, White Masks*. London: Pluto.
Fletcher, J. K. (1999). *Disappearing Acts – Gender, Power, and Relational Practice at Work*. Cambridge, MA: MIT Press.

Foucault, M., Bertani, M., Fontana, A., Ewald, F. O., and Macey, D. (2003). *Society Must Be Defended: Lectures at the College de France, 1975-76* (1st Picador pbk. edn). New York: Picador.

Foucault, M., and Sheridan, A. (1979). *Discipline and Punish: The Birth of the Prison*. Harmondsworth: Penguin.

Fraser, A. (2018). *Invisible: A Diary of Rough Sleeping in Britain*. London: Freedom Press.

Freedman, R. (1998). *Martha Graham, a Dancer's Life*. New York: Clarion Books.

Garcia, L. (1991). 'A short history of the Jingle dress'. *Crafts: American Indian: Past & Present*, 5 (Summer), pp. 14–16.

Gendlin, E. T. (1992). 'The primacy of the body, not the primacy of perception'. *Man and World*, 25(3), pp. 341–53. DOI: 10.1007/BF01252424

Goffman, E. (1980). *Behavior in Public Places: Notes on the Social Organization of Gatherings*. Westport, CT: Greenwood Press.

Gottlieb, R. (2008). *Reading Dance: A Gathering of Memoirs, Reportage, Criticism, Profiles, Interviews, and Some Uncategorizable Extras* (1st edn). New York: Pantheon Books.

Gottschild, B. D. (2003). *The Black Dancing Body: A Geography from Coon to Cool*. New York: Palgrave Macmillan.

Gould, S. J. (1996). *The Mismeasure of Man* (Rev. and expanded. ed.). New York; London: Norton.

Graham, M. (1991). *Blood Memory* (1st edn). New York: Doubleday.

Harvey, D. (2008). 'The right to the city'. *New Left Review*, 53, pp. 22–40.

Hegel, G. W. F., Dyde, S. W. B., and Ebrary, I. (2001). *Philosophy of Right* [electronic resource]. Kitchener, ON: Batoche.

Heidegger, M. (1989). *Hegel's Concept of Experience: With a Section from Helgel's Phenomenology of Spirit in the Kenley Royce Dove Translation* (1st Harper & Row pbk. edn). San Francisco: Harper & Row.

Heidegger, M. (2006). 'Building, dwelling, thinking'. In J. Morra and M. Smith (Eds), *Visual Culture: Critical Concepts in Media and Cultural Studies* (Vol. 3: Spaces of Visual Culture). London: Routledge.

Hildebrand, D. (2008). *Dewey: A Beginner's Guide*. Oxford: Oneworld.

Hillier, B. (1996). *Space is the Machine: A Configurational Theory of Architecture*. Cambridge: Cambridge University Press.

Holmes, R. (2008). *The Hottentot Venus: The Life and Death of Saartjie Baartman: Born 1789 – Buried 2002*. London: Bloomsbury.

Howes, D. (2005). *Empire of the Senses: The Sensual Culture Reader*. Oxford and New York: Berg.

Humphrey, D., and Pollack, B. (1979). *The Art of Making Dances*. London: Dance Books.

Ingold, T. (2000). *The Perception of the Environment: Essays on Livelihood, Dwelling and Skill*. London: Routledge.

Jackson, P. W. (1998). *John Dewey and Lessons of Art*. New Haven and London: Yale University Press.

Jonas, G. (1992). *Dancing: The Pleasure, Power, and Art of Movement*. New York: Hart N. Abrams in association with Thirteen/WNET.

LaMonthe, K. L., and Ebrary, I. (2006). *Nietzsche's Dancers: Isadora Duncan, Martha Graham, and the Revaluation of Christian Values*. New York: Palgrave Macmillan.

Lefebvre, H. (2004). *Rhythmanalysis: Space, Time, and Everyday Life*. London and New York: Continuum.

Lerman, L. (2011). *Hiking the Horizontal: Field Notes from a Choreographer*. Hanover, NH: Wesleyan University Press.

Lindley, D. (2007). *Uncertainty: Einstein, Heisenberg, Bohr, and the Struggle for the Soul of Science* (1st edn). New York and London: Doubleday.

Māhina, 'O. (2002). 'Atamai, fakakaukau and vale: "Mind", "thinking" and "mental illness" in Tonga'. *Pacific Health Dialog*, 9(2), pp. 303–308.

Māhina, 'O. (2004). *Art as Ta-Va 'Time-Space' Transformation*. Auckland, New Zealand: Center for Pacific Studies, University of Auckland.

Manning, E., and Massumi, B. (2014). *Thought in the Act: Passages in the Ecology of Experience*. Minneapolis and London: University of Minnesota Press.

Massey, D. B. (2005). *For Space*. London and Thousand Oaks, CA: Sage.

McFee, G. (1992). *Understanding Dance*. London: Routledge.

McHarg, I. L. (1969). *Design with Nature*. Garden City, NY: published for the American Museum of Natural History [by] the Natural History Press.

McKittrick, K. (2006). *Demonic Grounds: Black Women and the Cartographies of Struggle*. Minneapolis and London: University of Minnesota Press.

McKittrick, K. (2015). *Sylvia Wynter: On Being Human as Praxis*. Durhan: Duke University Press.

Merleau-Pont, M. (2002). *Phenomenology of Perception* (P. Kegan, Trans.). London and New York: Routledge.

Morgan, B. B. (1980). *Martha Graham, Sixteen Dances in Photographs* (1st rev. edn). Dobbs Ferry, NY: Morgan & Morgan.

New Lakota Dictionary: Lakhotiyapi-English / English-Lakhotiyapi & Incorporating the Dakota Dialects of Yankton – Yanktonai & Santee-Sisseton (2008). Bloomington, IN: Lakota Language Consortium.

Nikolais, A., and Louis, M. (2005). *The Nikolais/Louis Dance Technique: A Philosophy and Method of Modern Dance*. New York and London: Routledge.

Ogden, C. K., and Richard, I. A. (1989). *The Meaning of Meanng: A Study of the Influence of Language Upon Thought and of the Science of Symbolism*. San Diego: Harcourt Brace Jovanovich.

Pallasmaa, J. (2005). *The Eye of the Skin: Architecture and the Sense*. Chichester, Hoboken, NJ: Wiley-Academy; John Wiley & Sons.

Pink, S. (2011). 'From Embodiment to Emplacement: Re-thinking Competing Bodies, Sense and Spatialities'. *Sport, Education and Society*, 16(3), pp. 343–55.

Pratt, S. L. (2001). 'The given land: Black Hawk's conception of place'. *Philosophy and Geography*, 4(1), pp. 109–26.

Pratt, S. L. (2002). *Native Pragmatism: Rethinking the Roots of American Philosophy*. Bloomington, IN: Indiana University Press.

Putnam, R. D. (2000). *Bowling Alone: The Collapse and Revival of American Community*. New York and London: Simon & Schuster.

Rasmussen, S. E. (1959). *Experiencing Architecture* (Trans. Eve Wendt; 1st United States edn). Cambridge, MA: Technology Press of Massachusetts Institute of Technology.

Regensdorf, L. (2019). 'With a new dance series, Le Corbusier's villa Savoye becomes an unlikely stage'. *Vogue Magazine*. Retrieved from https://www.vogue.com/slideshow/le-corbusier-villa-savoye-dance-series

Sennett, R. (1994). *Flesh and Stone: The Body and the City in Western Civilization*. London: Faber.

Sharr, A. (2007). *Heidegger for Architects*. London: Routledge.

Sheets-Johnstone, M. (2009). *The Corporeal Turn: An Interdisciplinary Reader*. Exeter, UK and Charlottesville, VA: Imprint Academic.

Shilling, C. (2003). *The Body and Social Theory* (2nd ed ed.). London, Thousand Oaks, CA: SAGE Publications.

Sullivan, S. (2001). *Living Across and Through Skins: Transactional Bodies, Pragmatism and Feminism*. Bloomington: Indiana University Press.

Summerson, J., and Colvin, H. (2003). *Georgian London* (new edn). New Haven, CT and London: Yale University Press.

Synnott, A. (1993). *The body social : symbolism, self and society*. Routledge.

Tharp, T., and Reiter, M. (2006). *The Creative Habit: Learn It and Use It for Life: A Practical Guide* (1st Simon & Schuster pbk. edn). New York: Simon & Schuster.

Thomas, H. (2003). *The Body, Dance, and Cultural Theory*. Basingstoke: Palgrave Macmillan.

Thompson, K. D. (2014). *Ring Shout, Wheel About: The Racial Politics of Music and Dance in North American Slavery*. Urbana, Chicago, Springfield: University of Illinois Press.

Trask, H. K. (1993). *From a Native Daughter: Colonialism and Sovereignty in Hawai'i*. Monroe, ME: Common Courage Press.

Tufnell, M., and Crickmay, C. L. (2004). *A Widening Field: Journeys in Body and Imagination*. Alton: Dance.

Ward, C., White, D. F., and Wilbert, C. (2011). *Autonomy, Solidarity, Possibility: The Colin Ward Reader*. Edinburgh: AK.

Wellard, I. (Ed.) (2015). *Researching Embodied Sport: Exploring Movement Cultures*. London and New York: Routledge.

Wendt, A. (1999). 'Tautauing the Post-Colonial Body'. In V. Hereniko and R. Wilson (Eds), *Inside out: Literature, Cultural Politics, and Identity in the New Pacific*. Lanham, MD: Rowman & Littlefield Publishers, inc.

Whitehead, M. (Ed.) (2010). *Physical Literacy: Throughout the Lifecourse* (1st edn). London: Routledge.
Wilson, M. (1996). 'Black bodies/white cities: Le Corbusier in Harlem'. *ANY Architecture New York*, 16, pp. 35–9.
Winnicott, D. W. (2005). *Playing and Reality*. London: Routledge.
Wittgenstein, L., and Anscombe, G. E. M. (1953). *Philosophical Investigations*. New York: Macmillan.
Woodman, E. (2014). 'Le Corbusier burst into tears when he heard Josephine Baker sing "baby" – Ellis Woodman on architecture and dance'. *The Architectural Review*. Retrieved from https://www.architectural-review.com/8663569.article?sm=8663569.

ABOUT THE AUTHOR

Dr Adesola Akinleye, FHEA, FRSA, is a choreographer and artist-scholar. She began her career as a dancer with Dance Theatre of Harlem (USA), later working in UK dance companies such as Carol Straker Dance Company and Green Candle as well as running her own dance foundation in 2000s. She is founder and currently co-artistic director of DancingStrong Movement Lab. Over the past twenty years she has created dance works ranging from live performance that is often site-specific and involves a cross-section of the community, to dance films, installations and texts. Akinleye's work is characterized by an interest in voicing people's lived experiences in Place(s) through creative, moving portraiture. A key aspect of her process is the artistry of opening-up creative practices to everyone from ballerinas to women in low wage employment to performance for young audiences. She has won awards internationally for her choreographic work and is published in the areas of dance and cultural studies. She is a Senior Lecturer at Middlesex University, Theatrum Mundi Research Fellow, and visiting artist and Research Affiliate at MIT.

INDEX

aesthetic 7, 11–13, 15, 24, 28, 35, 53, 70, 87
   of becoming 106–8
   equity 113
Africanist 36, 45
agency 43, 123, 124
Akinleye, Adesola 6, 9, 12–13, 40, 49, 53, 64, 68, 73, 88, 89, 90, 93, 96, 114, 118, 123, 128–30
   Being-in-Place and Deweian experience xv
Alexander, Jake 76, 85, 94
American Indian traditions 38, 65
architectural theory 27
architecture 118, 120, 124
   performance of Self as 88–93
assemblage xiii, 8, 31, 32, 39, 59, 103–4, 112
audience, and dance 132

Baartman, Sarah 71–2, 105
ballet class 71–4
ballet dancer 114–15
Balz, Albert G. A. 31
Barthes, Roland 40
Bausch, Pina 81
Being-in-Place 111
   emplaced/embodied 65
   framework 23, 30–1, 40, 45, 65, 73, 83, 103, 118, 120
   situation of 40–2, 44
   somatic experience in 40–5
being present 35
Beyond Buildings: Performance as Architecture event 88–93

Bingham-Hall, John 27
   conversation with 101–8
Black xiii, xiv, 11, 43–5, 74, 129
   bodies 44, 72
Black dancing, hyper-invisibility in 94–7
Black female 45, 67, 68–9, 71, 72, 74, 105, 129
Black Hawk 37–8, 138, 141
Black Skin, White Masks (Fanon) 43–4
Blanchot, M. 20
Blood Memory (Graham) 33
bodily embodiment 36, 39, 40
body
   buildings and 42
   concept of 42
   on demonic grounds 70–1
   as machine 41, 51
   mind and 73
   space and 92
body–mind–environment 35, 40, 41
Bourdieu, Pierre 4
Boydston, J. A. 32
Brownian motion 77, 80
buildings 41–2, 45, 50–3, 63, 70, 101, 102, 105
Butler, J. 40

Califano, Anton 8, 49, 67
Casey, E. S. xvii–xix, 39
Chasing Stillness 49, 66, 70, 74, 75, 111, 112, 114, 115

choreographer   30
Choreographing the City project   1, 10, 11, 13, 16, 21, 23, 67, 76, 103, 106, 112, 113, 128
choreography   30
　choreo-thinking   17, 19
　defined   110
　design and   74
　languages   20–2
　making up dances   16–20
　place-making   19–20
　poems for   97–8
　questions   112–13, 116
choreo-thinking   17, 19
city art   102
Citybody   50–3, 104
　buildings   50–3
　as disembodied entity   52
　infrastructure   50–1
　mindfulness   51–2
　utilities   50–1
City Brain project   51
city-making   3, 5
classical/traditional dance   10, 13
collaboration   3–7, 12–13, 21, 22, 115, 128
communication   20, 33, 34
　knowledge   24
　non-verbal   24–5
　verbal   21, 23–6
community   84–6, 115, 129
　aesthetic   108
　city-making   3, 5
　collaboration   3–7, 12–13, 21, 115, 128
　dance arts   108
　togetherness   5–8
conjugate variables   112
contemporized dance   10, 13
corporeality   xix, 20, 39, 91
Cosgrave, Ellie   1, 13, 28–9, 52
Crickmay, Chris   35
cultural infrastructure   105

dance
　academy   114, 115
　audience and   132
　and choreography   16–19
　classical/traditional   11, 13
　contemporized   10, 13
　culture   3, 12, 108, 128
　and dancer   33
　defined   10
　embodied perspective   39
　fluidity of   10
　forms   113–14
　freedom in   13
　as interactions   13–15, 131
　languages   20–2
　on London Bridge   49, 67, 69
　movement   14–15, 17, 18, 23–4, 34, 35
　music and   121
　observer of   13–14, 18
　performance   108
　poems for   97–8
　stone   84–7
　studio   12, 59, 76, 80, 85, 129
　types   10, 13
dance-making   4, 5
dancer   13, 15, 16, 30, 32, 33, 56, 114, 115
　hyper-invisibility of Black female   94–7
　professional/trained   15, 16, 131
　stillness of   124
Deleuze, Gilles   41, 51
demonic design   72
demonic grounds   70–1, 96
Demonic Grounds: Black Women And The Cartographies Of Struggle (McKittrick)   68–9, 96
Design with Nature (McHarg)   27
Desire Lines   74, 97–8, 103
Dewey, John   xvii, 7, 25, 30, 32, 65, 103, 107, 119, 121

Being-in-Place framework 118
experience xv–xvi
language xiv
lived transactional
  experience 44–5
mindful-body 32–6, 51–2, 73
pragmatism 25, 30, 36–7
situation 31–2, 35, 39, 42, 43, 63
transaction 31, 34–5, 44, 131
dif-abilities. *See* disabilities
disabilities xvi, 129, 130
Donnelly, Aoife 19, 27, 28
double consciousness 43–4
DuBois, W. E. B. 43–4
dwelling 75–6, 85, 87, 94, 114–15
  as willing incompleteness 82–4
dwell time 53–4, 56

earth-hovering 79
Elements of Rhythmanalysis (Lefebvre) 39
embodied experience 92, 107, 112
embodied moving 6, 34
embodiment xvii, 34, 36–40, 51, 107
  [...] xx, 6, 7, 10, 17, 23, 26, 30, 34, 75, 82, 84, 92, 102, 121
  bodily 36, 39, 40
  mindful body-environment xiv, xvi, xviii, xix, 52, 65, 66, 92
  soma-centered xix, 21
emplacement xvii, 40, 91
environment 3–4, 18–20, 26–30, 35–40, 42, 52, 69, 83, 85, 86, 91, 104–7
epistemology 30, 32
Eric (pseudonym) 50–8, 76–81, 104
events
  Beyond Buildings: Performance as Architecture 88–93

  Golden Jubilee Bridge and Watford Way 94–7, 107
  Helen Kindred rehearsal 6, 40
  London Bridge 55, 56, 65–7, 69, 128
  Piccadilly 71–2
  street near British Library 93
  top of the escalator at waterloo station 57–8, 73
experience (Dewey) xiv–xvi, 31, 35, 36, 65, 103, 120

Fanon, Frantz
  Black Skin, White Masks 43–4
  Negro on the train 43–4, 96
fearful stillness 59
femininity 44–5
flow 3, 4, 39, 53, 62, 66, 68, 73
fluid boundaries 10, 12
foreground 18, 65
Foucault, Michel 4, 40
Fraser, Andrew 61–3, 68, 83, 95–6, 117, 124
Freedman, Russell 34
frightening noise 44
Fulleylove, Harry 22, 49, 64, 67–8, 76, 90–4, 107

geographyless 69
Georgian London (Summerson) 27
'Given Land: Black Hawk's conception of place, The' (Pratt) 37–8
'good enough' 120
Gottschild, Brenda Dixon 4
Graham, Martha 34
  Blood Memory 33
  'unity' of the movement of dance 35
Guattari, Felix 41, 51

Hard Rock Café 72

Harvey, D. 29
Heisenberg's Uncertainty Principle 111–12
Hejduk, John 87
homelessness 60–2, 67, 68, 96, 109
hovering 80–2, 85, 87, 114–15
Howes, D. xvii, 40
hyper-invisibility 94–7
hypervisibility 90

identity 40–5, 68–9, 72, 74, 96, 102–4
  in transaction 37
improvisation 84–6, 108
incompleteness xviii, 81, 90. *See also* unfinished
  becoming 106–8
  willing 82–4
indigenous 36, 45, 47, 73
indigenous American philosophy 37
information technology 52
infrastructure 50, 102–5, 108
Ingold, T. 137
intellectual experience 35
interactions 37–8
  of dance 14–15
interconnectedness 1, 3, 33, 47, 99
interdisciplinary 3, 5, 7, 10, 17, 18, 27, 30, 103
invisibility 96, 103. *See also* hyper-invisibility
Isadora programme 64, 89–90, 93, 97

Jewish community 116

Kindred, Helen 6, 10, 40, 80

Lakota 30, 45
landscapes of opportunity 84–7
language xiv, 20–2, 25, 26, 105–6, 114, 115
Larry (pseudonym) 51, 52, 58
Lavine, T. Z 32
Lee, N. 10
Lefebvre, Henri 39
Lerman, Liz 99, 113–16
  conversation with 109–10
  use of Heisenberg's Uncertainty Principle 111–12
lingering 87, 111
Lingering in Dwelling 75, 97, 111, 112
lived transactional experience 44–5
Logic of Place 37–8, 66–7, 107
London Bridge 55, 56, 65–6, 69, 128
  slowness and stillness 56
Louis, Murray 15, 35
luxury 60, 70

McFee, G. 10
McGonagle, Lauren 64, 76
McHarg, Ian 27
Mcintyre, Dianne 126–31
McKittrick, Katherine
  Black feminist approach 71–2
  demonic grounds 70, 96
  Demonic Grounds: Black Women And The Cartographies Of Struggle 68–9
making up dances 16–20, 26
Manning, Erin 25
Martha Graham: A Dancer's Life (Freedman) 34
Massey, D. B. 39, 41
Massumi, Brian 25
Merleau-Ponty, Maurice 38
mind-ful-body
  Dewey, John 32–6, 51–2, 73
  in transaction 32–6
mind-ful body–environment xiv, xvi, xviii, xix, 52, 65, 66, 92
misogyny 129

moment(s) xviii, 7, 23–4, 31–3, 35, 42–5, 59–63, 65, 82–6, 89, 118–20, 122–4, 131
   of stillness 73, 74
momentum 111–12
movement 14–15, 17, 18, 23–6, 30, 34, 119, 123–5
movement-paper soundtrack
   first part of 91–2
   second part of 92–3
moving body 4
multiplicity 90, 104, 106
mySelf xix, 5, 6, 76, 83, 91, 105

Native American philosophy 36
Native Pragmatism (Pratt) 36
Nikolais, Alwin 15, 35
nimble ability 112, 114
nimble thinking 111
noise 31–2
non-commercial waits 56
non-dancer 15–16
non-verbal communication 24–5
non-verbal knowledge 17–21, 24. *See also* verbal knowledge
norm, sense of 45
nowness xx, 31, 44, 65, 69, 102, 105, 132

observer, of dance 13–14, 18
Ogden, C. K. 9
ontology 30, 32
opportunity landscapes 84–7
otherness 67, 70–1, 73, 102, 128, 129

park 60
Parthasarathy, Sowmya 27, 59–62, 84
performances
   Beyond Buildings performance, Royal Academy of Arts (17 May 2019) 88–93

   Re:generations, The Lowey (9 November 2019) 19
   of Self 88–93
   sharing at Royal Academy of Arts (28 September 2019) 8
   sharing at The Place (20 April 2019) 19
   technical structure of 97
permeable 80–1, 97, 114, 115
Petichta 115
physical literacy 17–18, 21
Pink, Sarah xvii, 40
Place xvii, xviii, 12, 18, 37, 39–40, 43, 44, 49, 62, 66–7, 70, 72–6, 91, 96, 105–7, 110–12
   assemblage 103, 104
   of Being-in-Environment 92
   polyrhythms of 75, 83, 86
   rhythms of 96
place-making 3, 5, 19–20, 63
poems 97–8
polyrhythms xix, 75, 83
pragmatism 40
   Dewey, John 25, 30, 36–7
Pratt, Scott L. xvii, 39, 65
   'Given Land: Black Hawk's conception of place, The' 37–8
   Logic of Place 66–7
   Native Pragmatism 36
professional dancers 15, 16
public art 56, 102
Putnam, Bob (Robert) 116

queer 68, 69, 96, 128, 129

race 129
racism 69, 129
Radlowska-Judd, Maga 22, 67–8, 76, 94, 107
Rasmussen, S. E. 34, 38–9
realities 103

reflexivity 4, 7, 14–15
rehearsal 67, 84, 85, 119
rehearsal rhythm 81
relationships xviii, 3, 18, 19, 29, 30, 49, 65–70, 72–5, 81, 82, 85, 87, 91, 94, 96, 97, 101, 103, 120, 122, 124, 128
  rhythm and 104–5, 110–12
  transactional xvi, 32, 65, 101
Residing in Wandering 75, 97, 111, 112
rhythm 3, 26, 32, 39, 40, 49, 65–70, 73–6, 83–7, 91, 94, 96, 105
  of identity 96
  movements 81
  and relationships 104–5, 110–12
  of sunrise 67
  of walk-to-work 69
Richard, I. A. 9
Rite of Spring (Bausch) 81
Roberts, Terry (pseudonym) 29, 53–8, 76–9, 82, 127

Self xvii, xix, 4, 30, 31, 38, 40, 41, 45, 75, 82–3, 85, 88, 103, 110
  performance of 88–93
self-identity 38, 45, 128
'Self-in-body' 11
Sennett, Richard 117–25
sensations 6, 14, 15, 18, 21, 34, 35, 70
sense of norm 45
sensing body 35, 56
sexism 69
shadowless sensation 6, 40
Sheets-Johnson, Maxine 4, 24
silence, stillness and 122–5
site/sight xix, 19, 21, 24
site-specific dance 82
situation xvi, 30, 37, 83, 103, 108
  of Being-in-Place 40–2, 44
  description 31

Dewey, John 31–2, 35, 39, 42, 43, 63
Situationist 86
slowness, on London Bridge 55
somatic xix, 10, 11, 17–22, 26
  somatic-based perspective xix, 22
  somatic experience, Being-in-Place in 40–5
sound 122–4
space 11, 18, 91, 92, 110
spatial acts of presence 65–6
spontaneous composition 131–2
stages 18
stillness. *See also Chasing Stillness*
  connection 63–4, 69
  conversation on waiting 53–6
  fearful 58
  of home 76–80
  hypervisibility 90
  on London Bridge 55
  as luxury 60, 70
  as mindful body 62
  moments of 73, 74
  and movement 60, 64
  nature of 111
  as otherness 67, 70–1, 73
  of the place 61
  as presence 65–6
  qualities of 59–63
  and silence 121–4
  street dancing 64–5
stone dancing 84–7
street dancing 64–5, 67–8
Summerson, John 27

Tā/Vā 73, 110–11
Tarrio, Nicole 28
temporality 11, 43
Theatrum Mundi xii, 98, 99, 128
Thought in the Act: passages in the ecology of experience (Manning and Massumi) 25
time 11, 18, 110

temporality xix, 11, 43
togetherness 5–8
trained dancers 15. *See also* professional dancers
transaction xvi, 31–2, 38–42, 83
   Dewey, John 31, 34–5, 44, 131
   of embodiment 107
   identity in 37
   lived experience of 44–5
   mind-ful-body in 32–6
   situation of 103
trans community 116
Trommer, Kristin 19, 27
Tufnell, Miranda 35

unfinished 104–6
un-geographic 68–9, 72–3, 128
unrealities 103
un-rhythmic 69
urban design 42, 45, 104, 106, 108
urbanism 104, 106, 108
urbanization 28–9
us-ness 110–13

utilities 50

Valentine's Park 61
Vasilikou, Carolina 12, 82, 87
verbal communication 21, 23–5
verbal knowledge 17, 21, 25
verbal language xiv, 25, 26

waiting 53–6
wandering 75–80, 85, 86, 94, 96, 111. *See also Residing in Wandering*
   as willing incompleteness 82–4
Ward, Colin 28
water-hovering 81
Wellard, Ian 4
Western dance 11
whenness 117–25
white 102, 129. *See also* Black
Whitehead, Margaret 17–18, 21
Widening Field, A (Tufnell and Crickmay) 35
window shade 43–4

Yoruba 30

www.ingramcontent.com/pod-product-compliance
Lightning Source LLC
Chambersburg PA
CBHW070642300426
44111CB00013B/2216